Kumon Creative Doodling Workbooks

My Awesome Doodle & Draw Workbook

Parent's Guide

This book uses a carefully structured, step-by-step approach that allows your child to have fun and build confidence while developing creativity and problem-solving skills. To help your child get the maximum benefit from this book, we recommend the following:

- Have your child start at the beginning of the book and complete the activities in order, rather than skipping around.
- Encourage your child to have fun. Let him or her know that there is no single correct response.
- Allow your child to draw things from his or her imagination as well as real-life things and events.
- Refer to the sample responses on page 128 if your child needs additional guidance.
- Limit the number of pages your child completes in a day so he or she still wants to do a little more at the end of each session.

The "To parents" notes throughout this book provide more comments and advice on how to support your child as he or she completes the activities.

You will notice that the activities in this book become more challenging as your child progresses through them. A primary goal of the book is to prepare your child to complete the problem-solving activities at the end of the book. The activities in the book are grouped in the following six sections:

(1) Coloring: The coloring tasks help build confidence and introduce your child to the format of the book. To begin, your child will use only one designated color. As your child progresses through this section, he or she will use more colors and also make his or her own color choices.

(2) Decorating: The decorating tasks involve drawing patterns. To begin, your child will copy one pattern shown in the picture. As your child progresses, he or she can choose from various patterns to copy and also design his or her own patterns.

(3) Drawing Something Specific: In these activities, your child will add something to the picture. The directions give specific information about what to add. To begin, your child can copy examples shown in the picture. Later on, the activities encourage your child to exercise more creativity in choosing what to draw and how to draw it.

(4) Drawing with Shapes: In these activities, your child will turn shapes into a variety of different objects. As your child progresses through the section, he or she will exercise more creativity in choosing what to draw and how to draw it.

(5) Drawing Something Creative: These activities require more creativity and decision-making ability than the previous tasks. Your child will decide what to add to each picture with little direction from the instructions. It is important for your child to recognize that there is no single correct response for each task.

(6) Problem Solving: In these activities, each picture shows a problem. Your child will add something to the picture to solve the problem. To complete these tasks, your child will draw on the creativity, fine motor skills, and decision-making abilities that he or she has been practicing throughout the book.

Coloring
Harvest Apples

■ Color the apples.

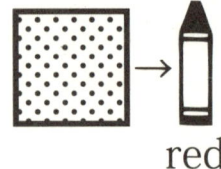 → red

To parents: This book contains several different activity types that gradually increase in difficulty. The first activity type is coloring. Guide your child to color the areas that have a pattern.

Toy Poodle

■ Color the lion cubs.

yellow

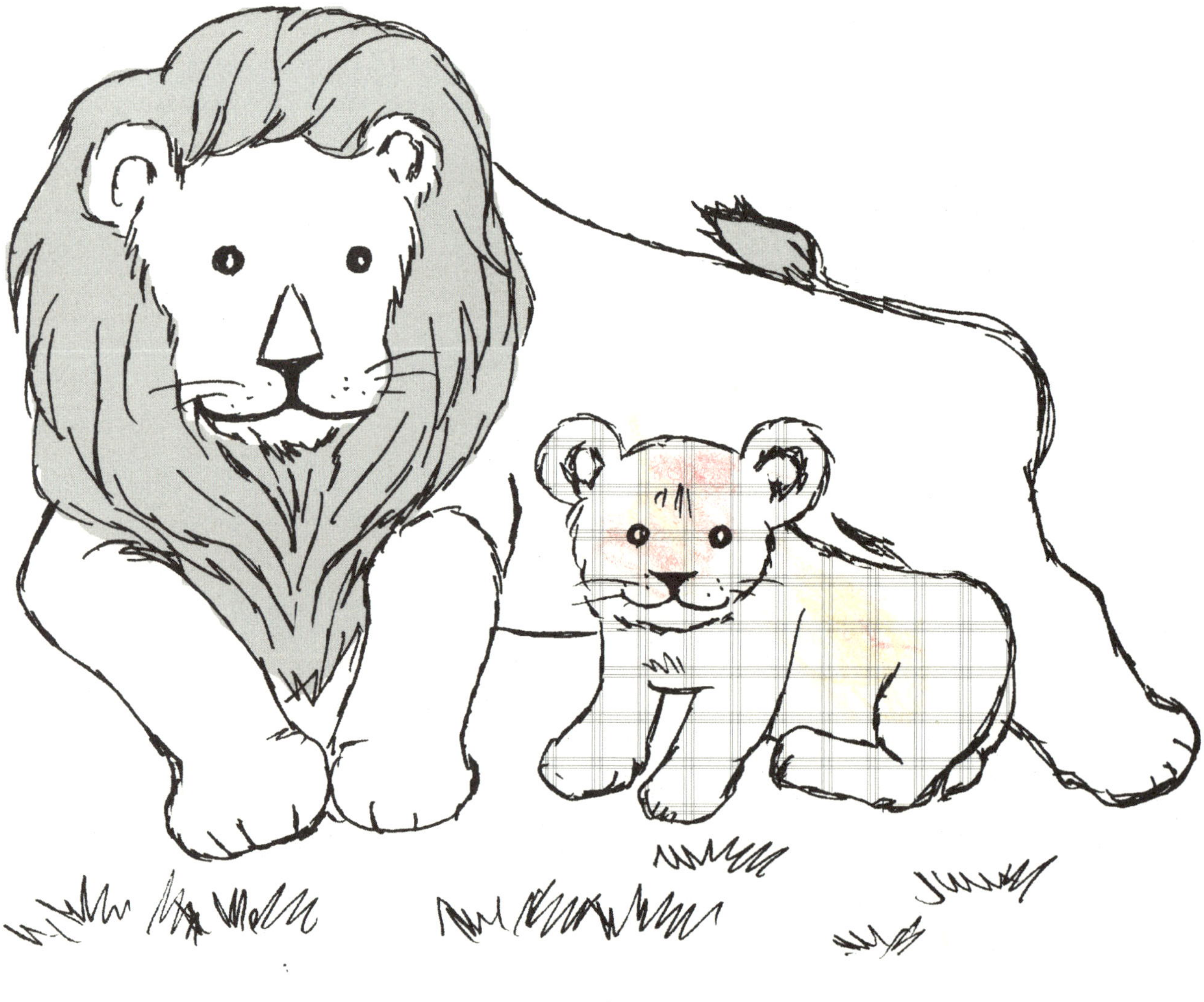

To parents: The first coloring activities in this book use only one color. This beginning-level task helps to build your child's confidence and familiarity with the book.

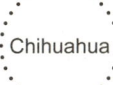

Chihuahua

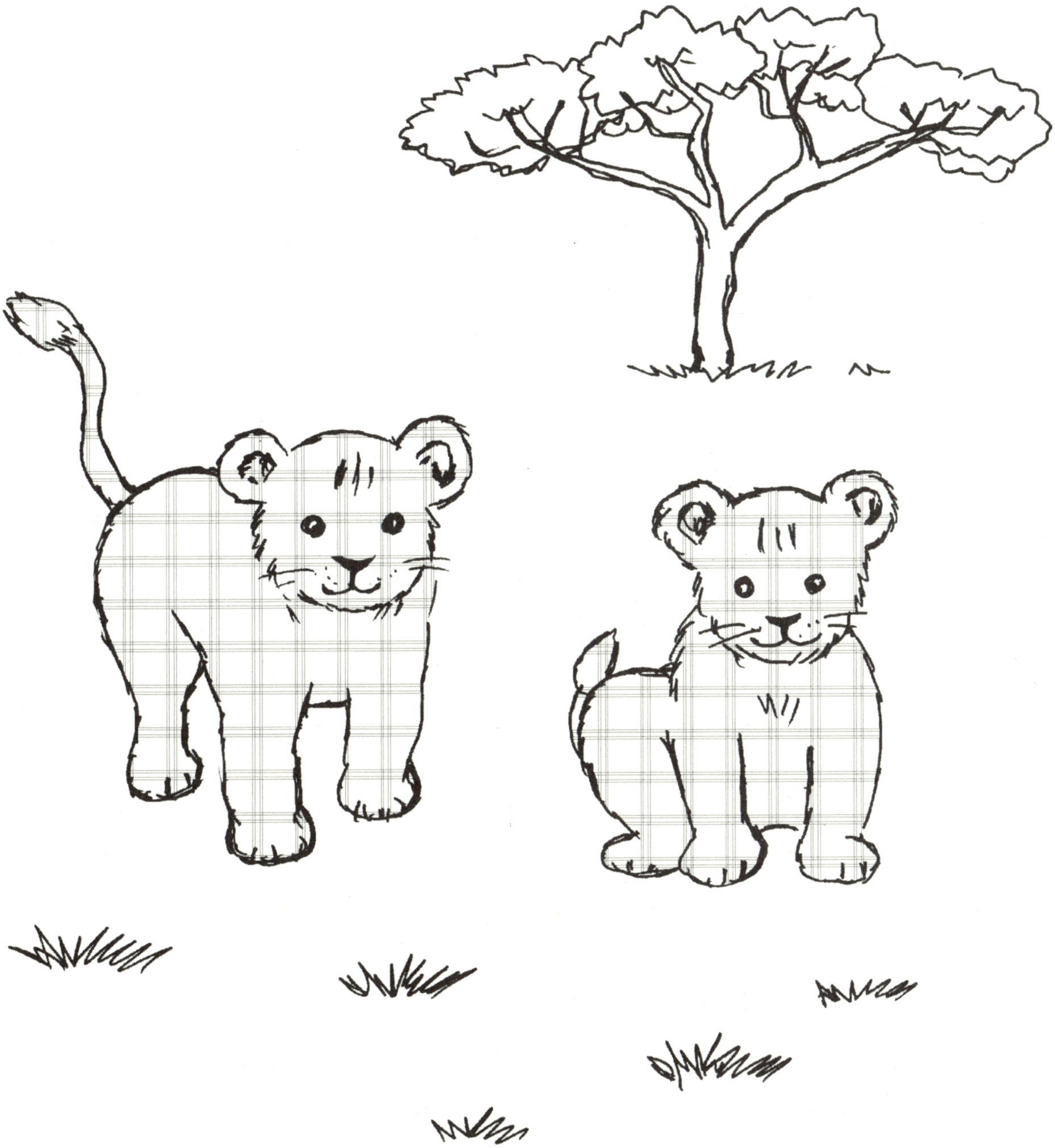

Coloring
Bon Appétit

Color the steaks.

brown

To parents: Many children enjoy pretending to cook. With this activity your child can pretend to be making steaks.

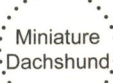

Miniature Dachshund

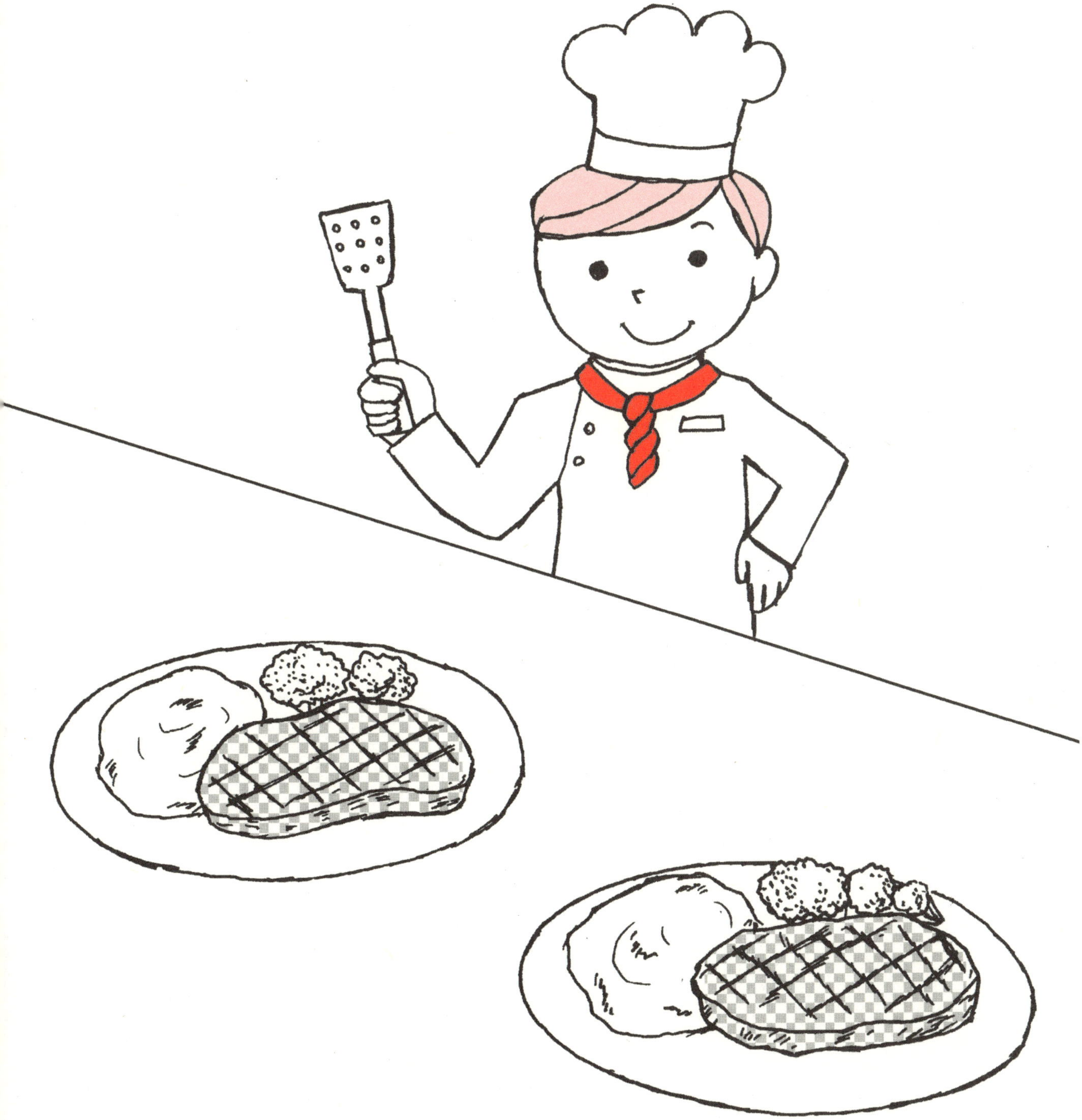

Coloring
Fruit Bowl

■ Color the bananas and oranges.

yellow   orange

To parents: The coloring is now more challenging because more than one color is used.

Pomeranian

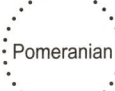

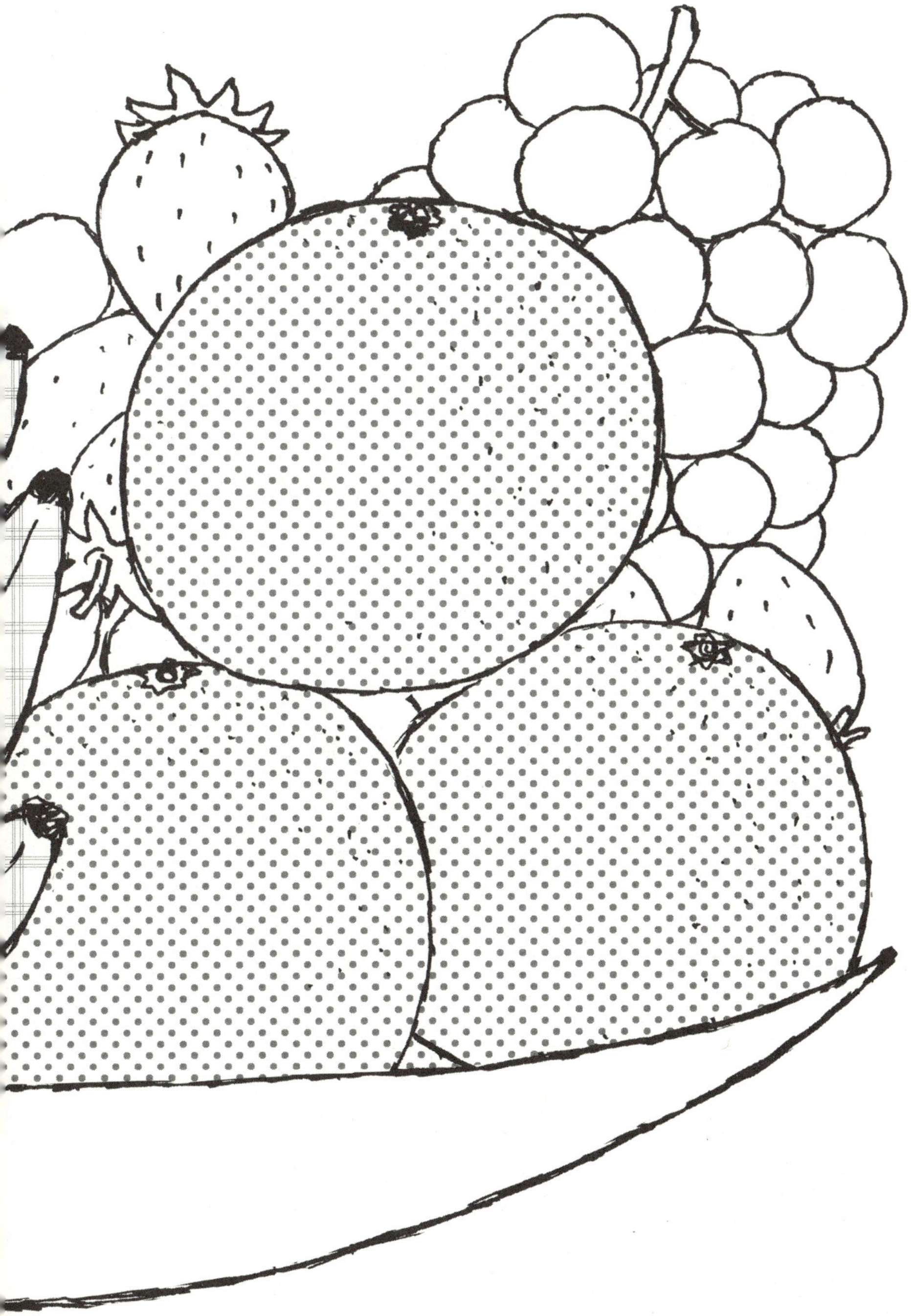

Coloring
Flower Bed

■ Color the sunflowers and roses.

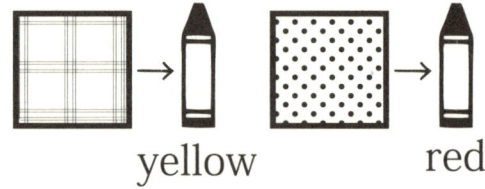

yellow   red

To parents: You may wish to help your child locate the roses and sunflowers in the picture.

Yorkshire
Terrier

11

Coloring
Safari Park

■ Color the alligators and hippos.

green   brown

To parents: You may need to help your child understand which color to use with which pattern.

Shiba Inu

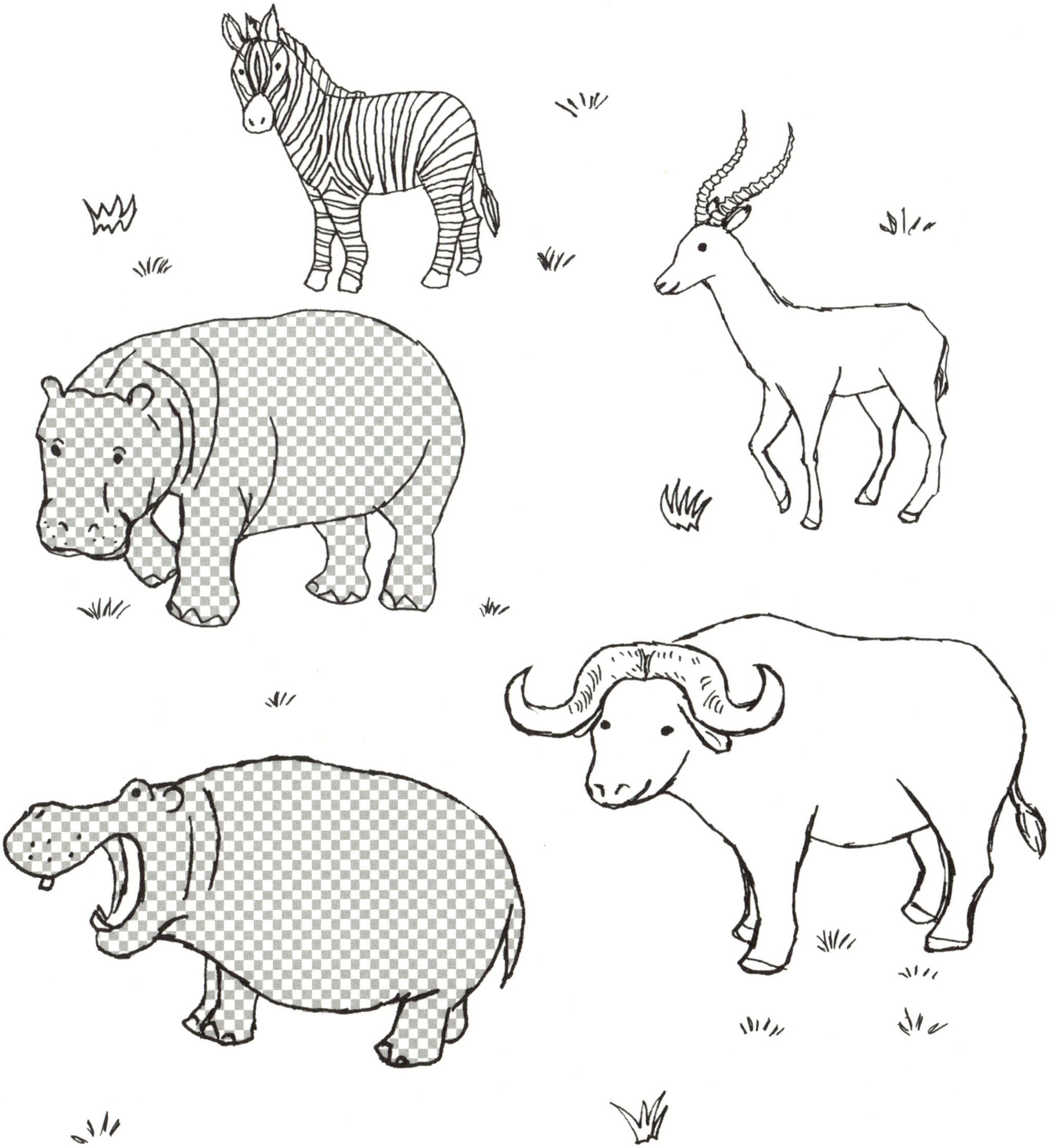

Coloring
Tropical Birds

■ Color the tropical birds as you like.

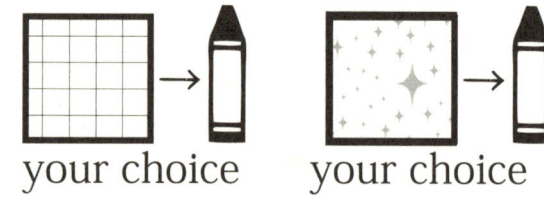

your choice   your choice

To parents: Starting with this activity, your child can choose which color or colors to use. Encourage your child to have fun and be creative.

Miniature Schnauzer

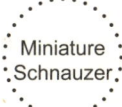

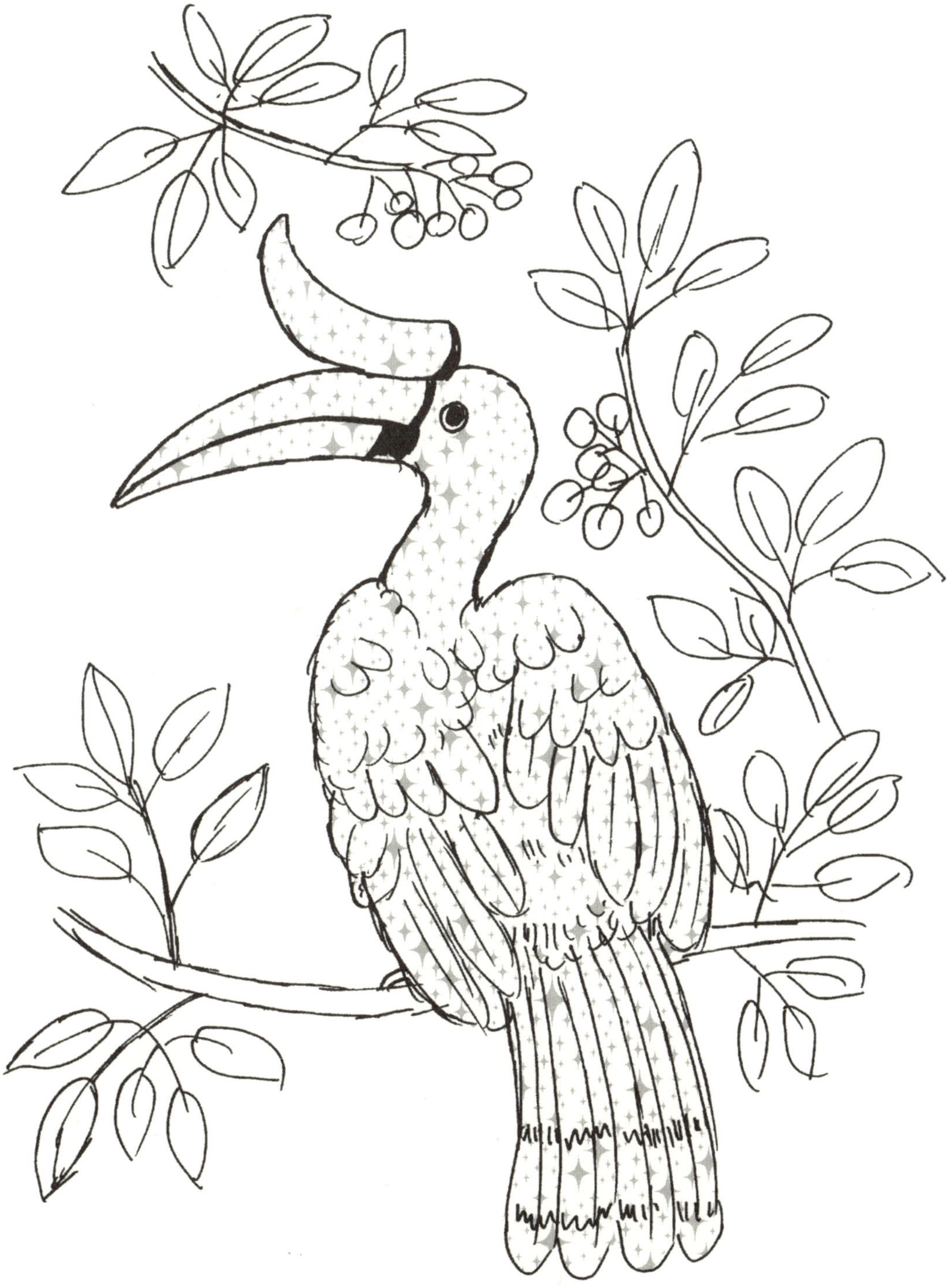

Coloring
Beams from a Lighthouse

■ Color the beams of light.

your choice

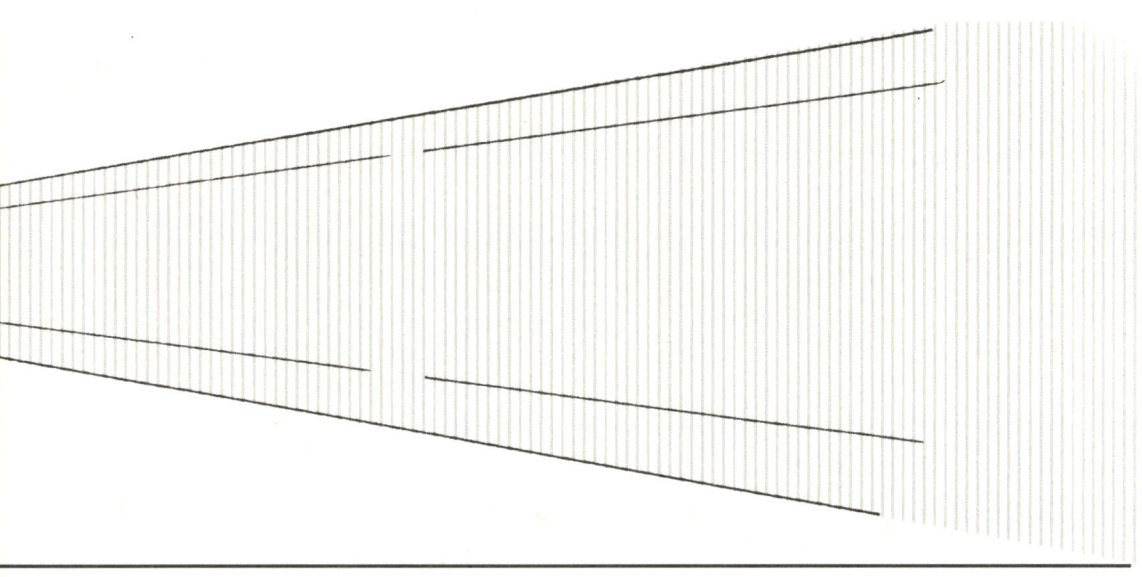

Coloring
All Dressed Up

◼ Color the hats.

your choice

To parents: Your child can use the same color for all four hats or different colors.

Maltese

Coloring
Towers of Toy Blocks

■ Color the toy blocks.

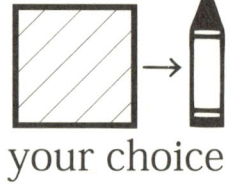

your choice

To parents: For an added challenge, encourage your child to use several different colors.

Beagle

11 Decorating
Missing Stripes

One of the tigers is missing some stripes. Can you help?

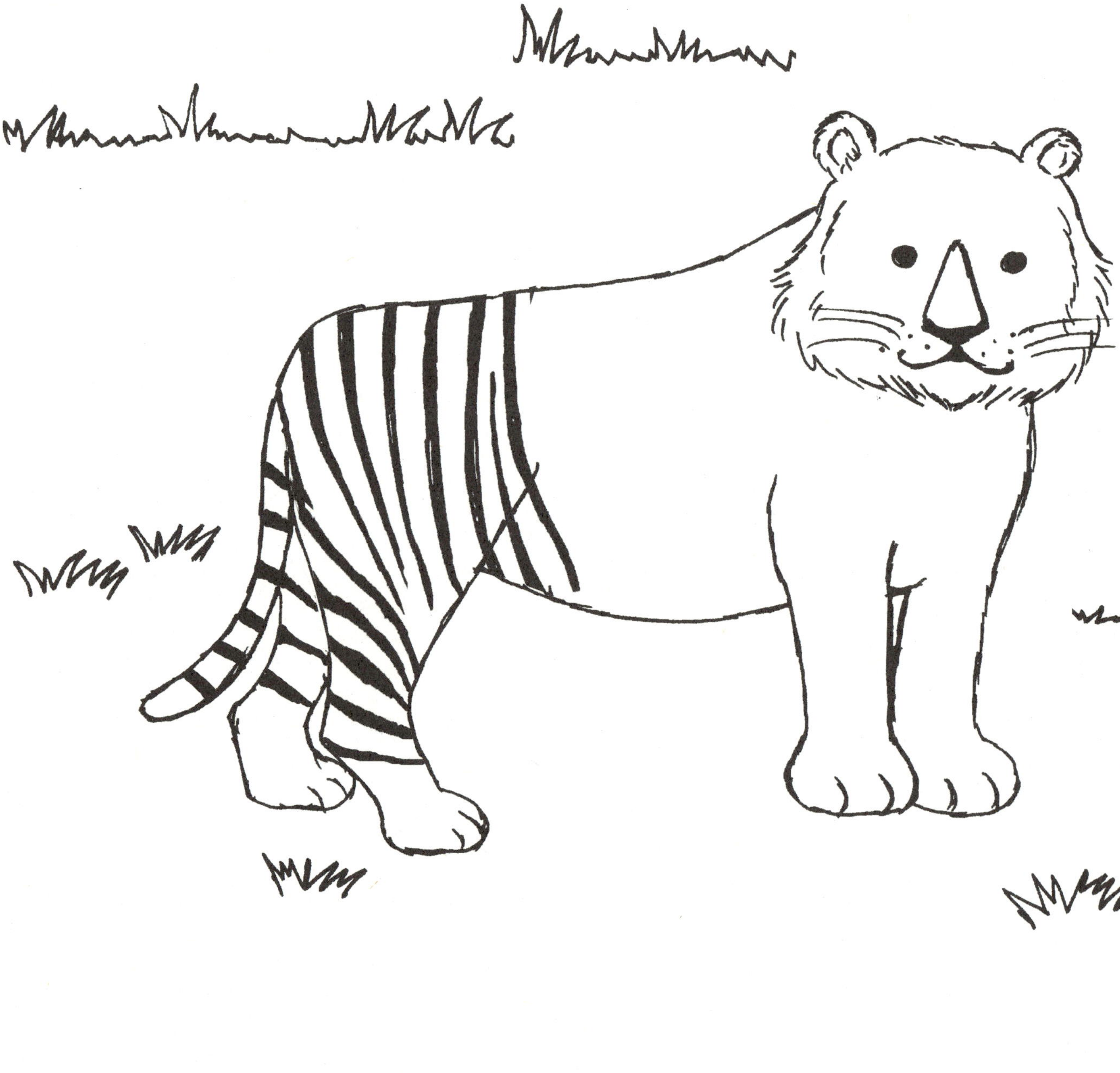

To parents: If your child has difficulty, point out which tiger is missing some of its stripes.

Kaninchen
Dachshund

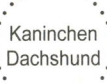

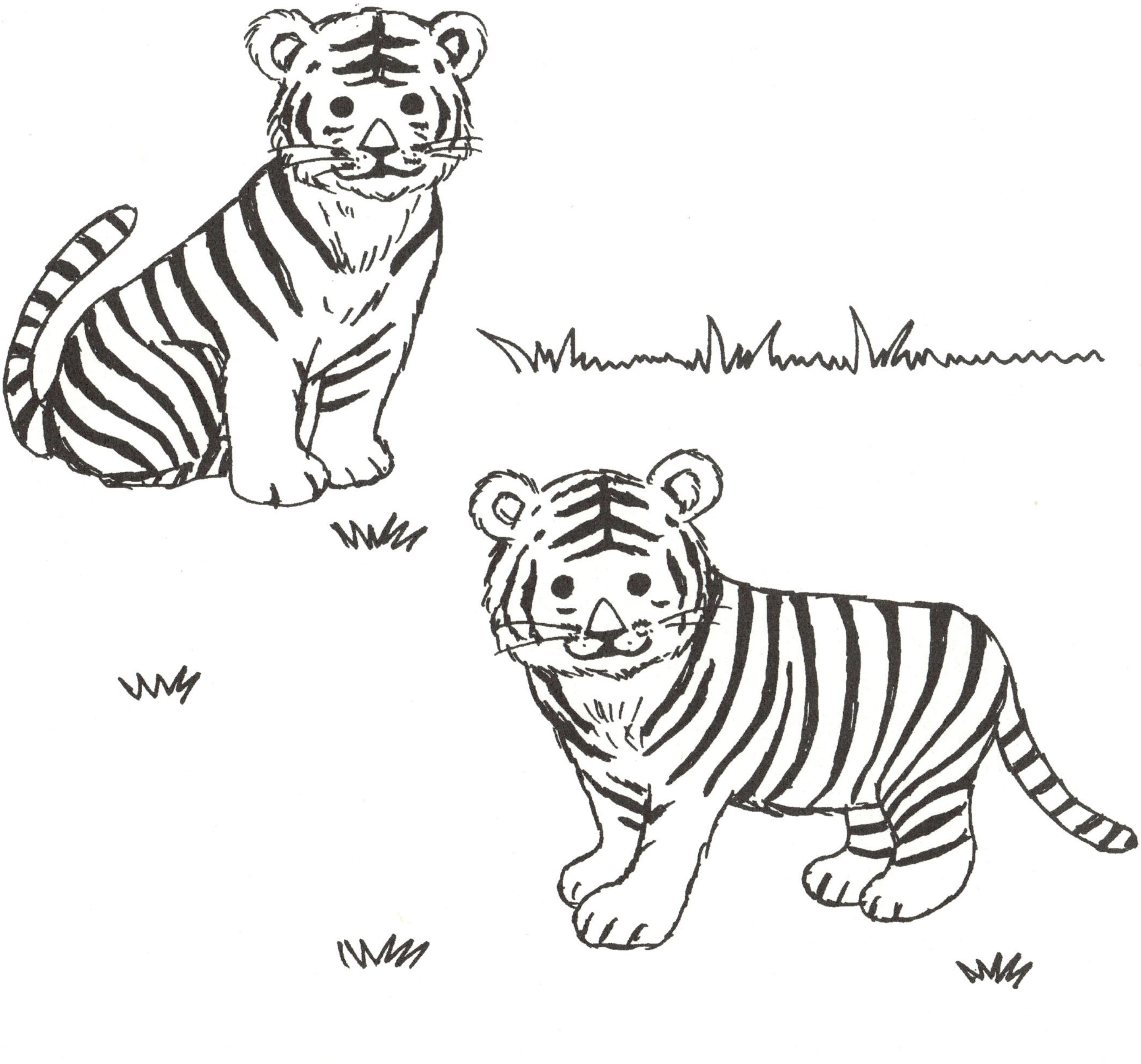

12 Decorating
Missing Spots

Some of the giraffes are missing some spots. Can you add them?

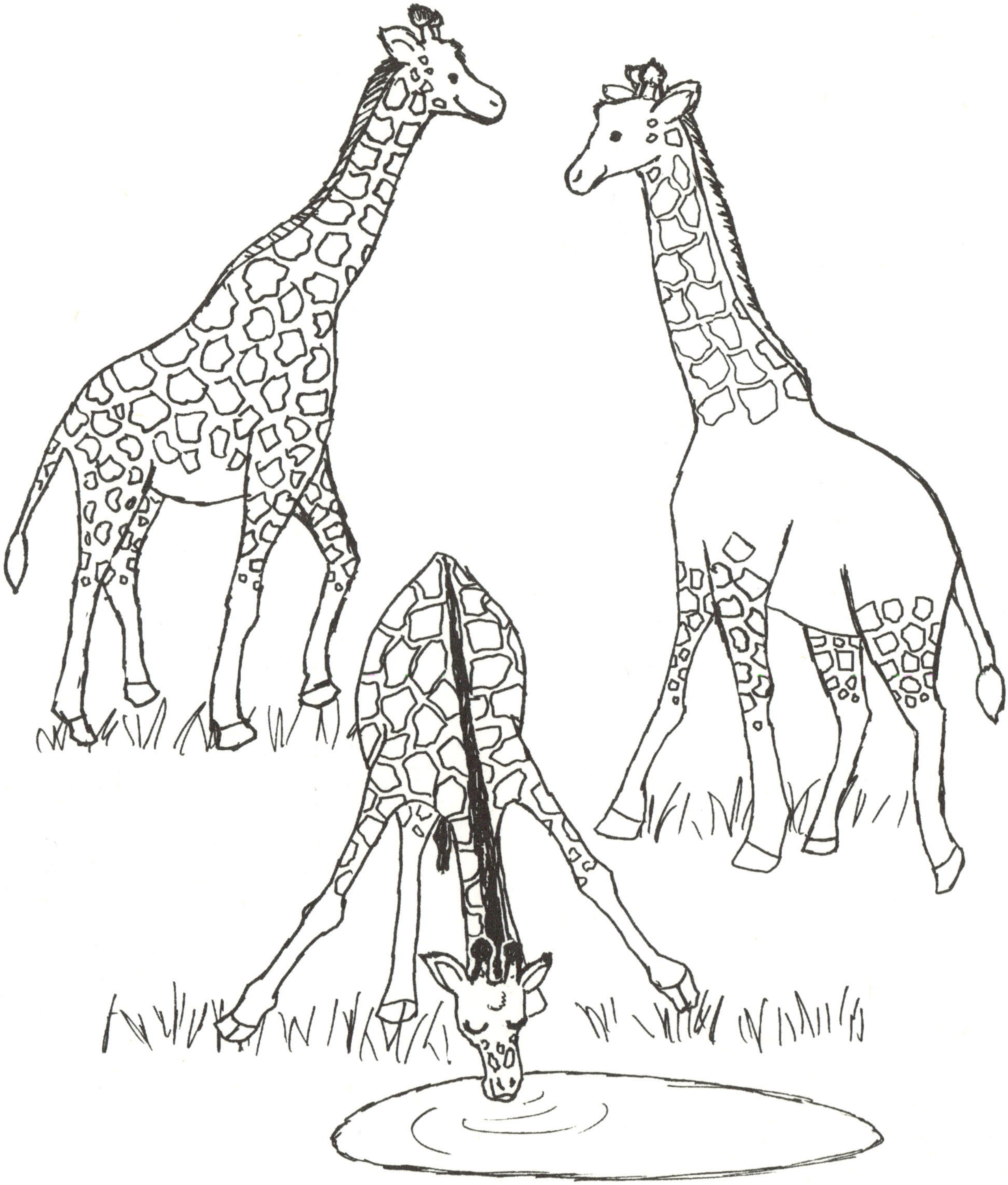

To parents: Encourage your child to look at the spots on the other giraffes before he or she begins drawing.

13 Decorating
Waves on Plates

Can you decorate the last plate?

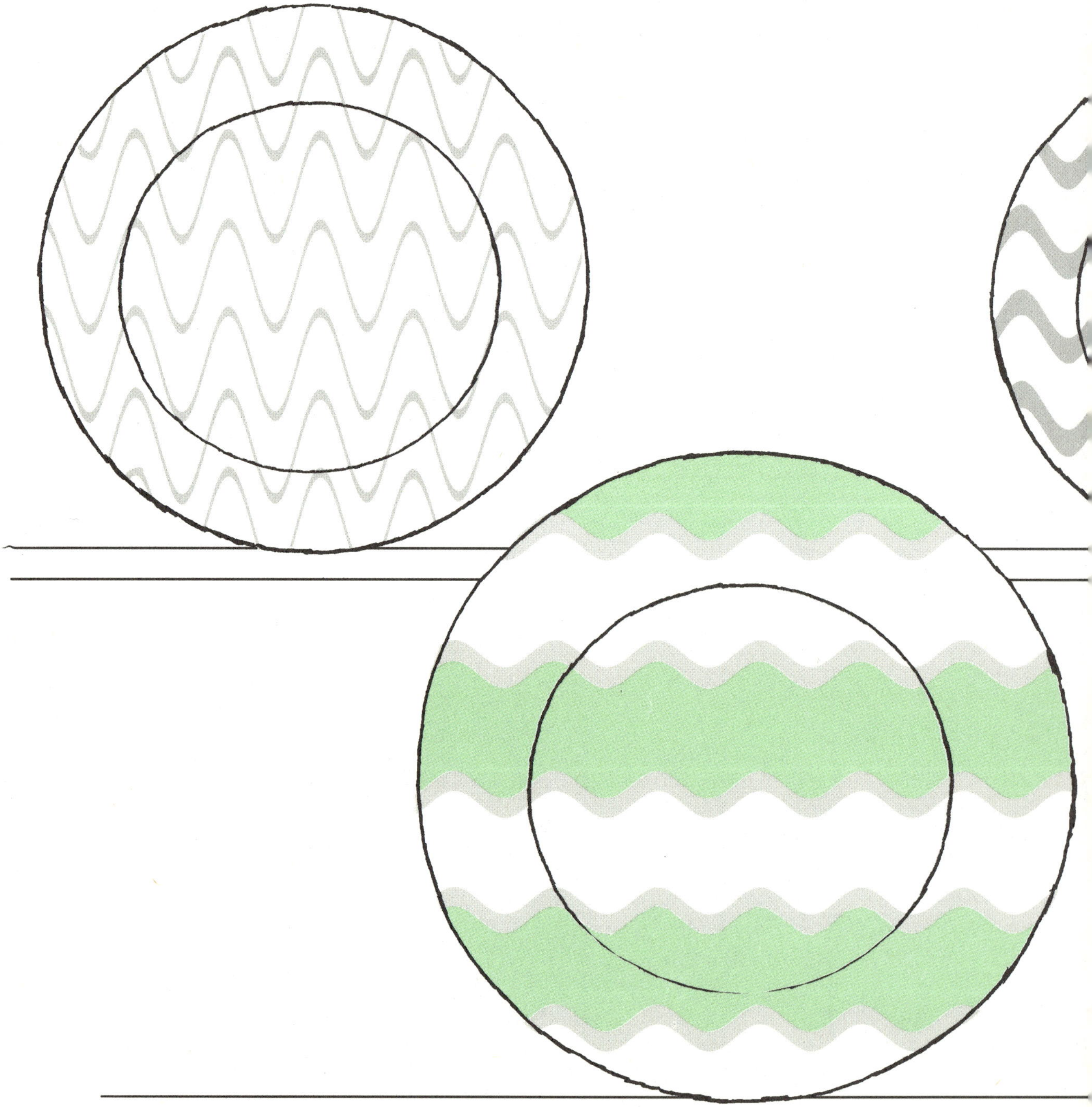

To parents: If your child has difficulty, ask him or her to describe the pattern on the other plates.

Pembroke Welsh Corgi

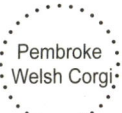

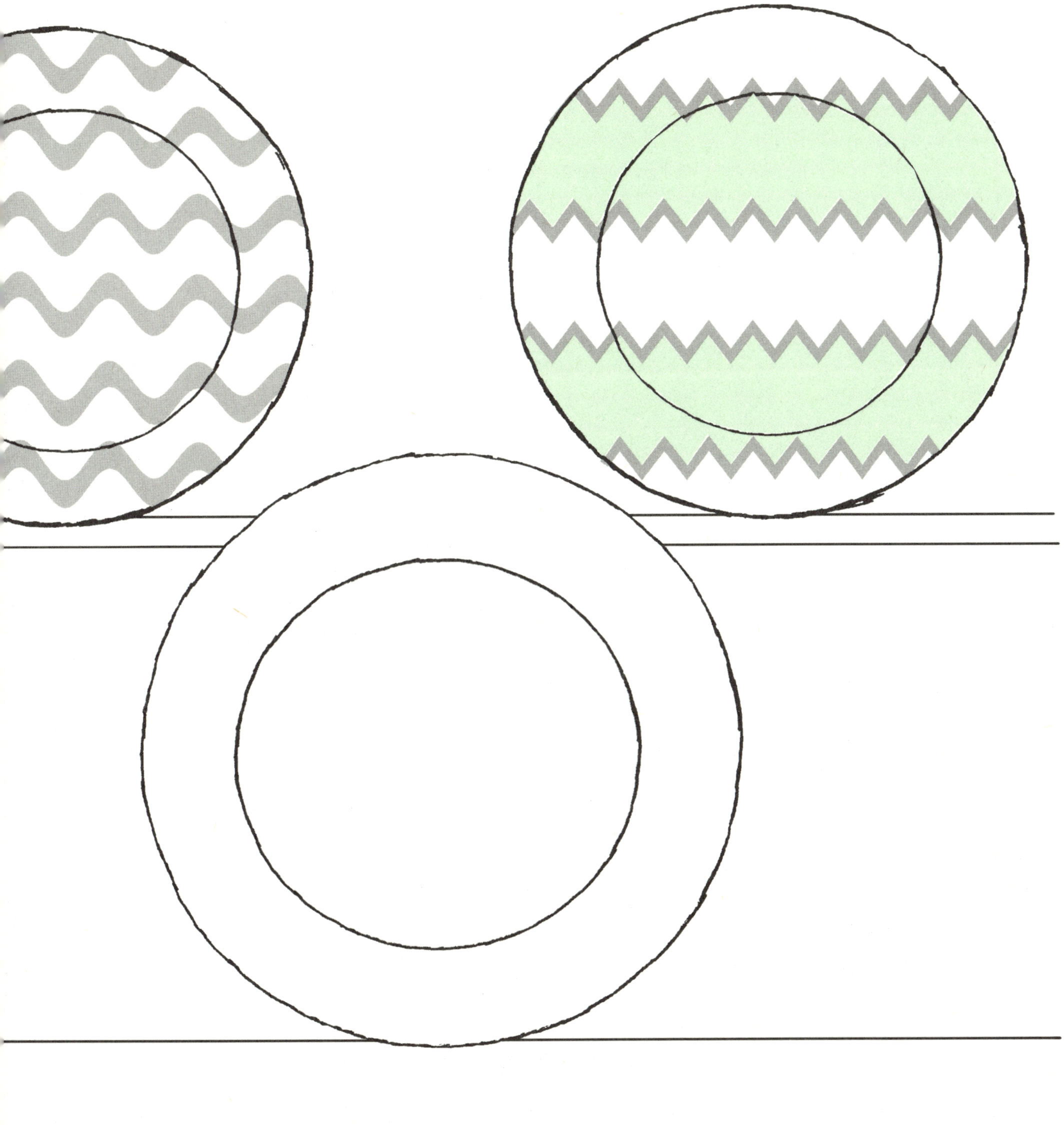

14 Decorating
Racing Flag

Decorate the flag. Be sure to be checkered pattern.

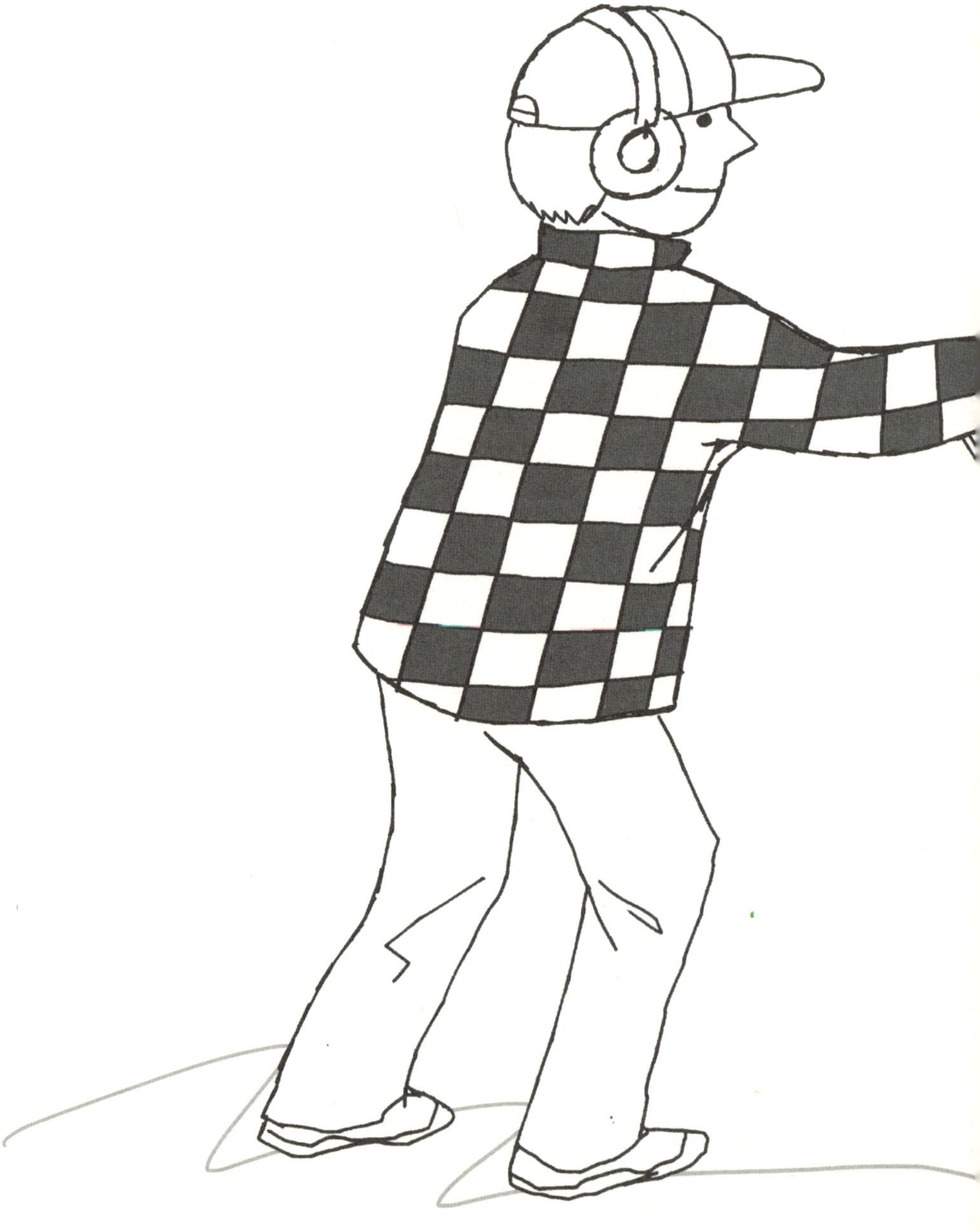

Pug

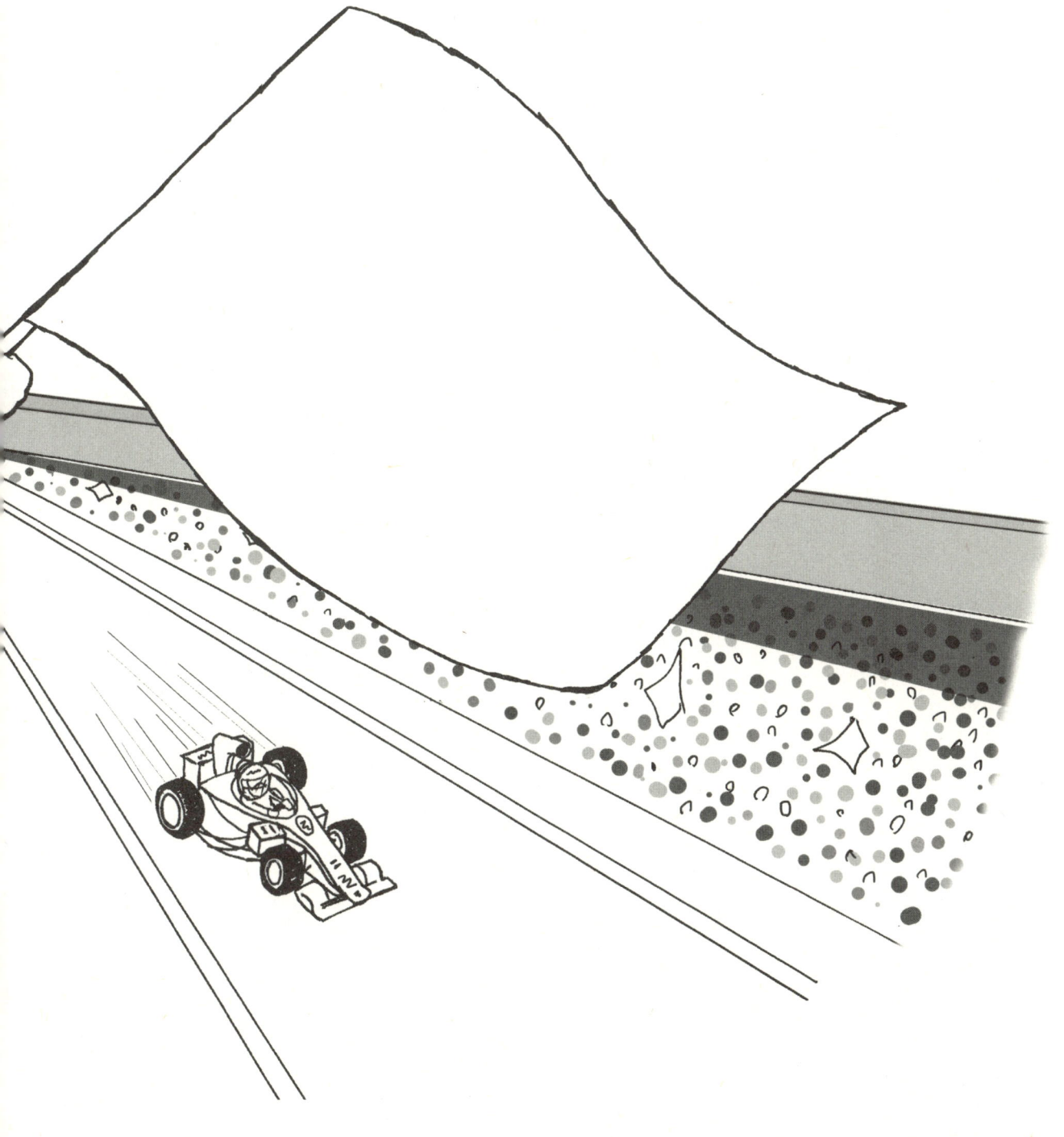

One of the cards is missing a pattern. Can you decorate it?

Pekingese

THANK YOU

thank you

16 Decorating
Laundry Day

■ Decorate the pants and towel.

To parents: Your child can use the same pattern on the pants and towel or two different patterns.

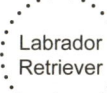

Labrador Retriever

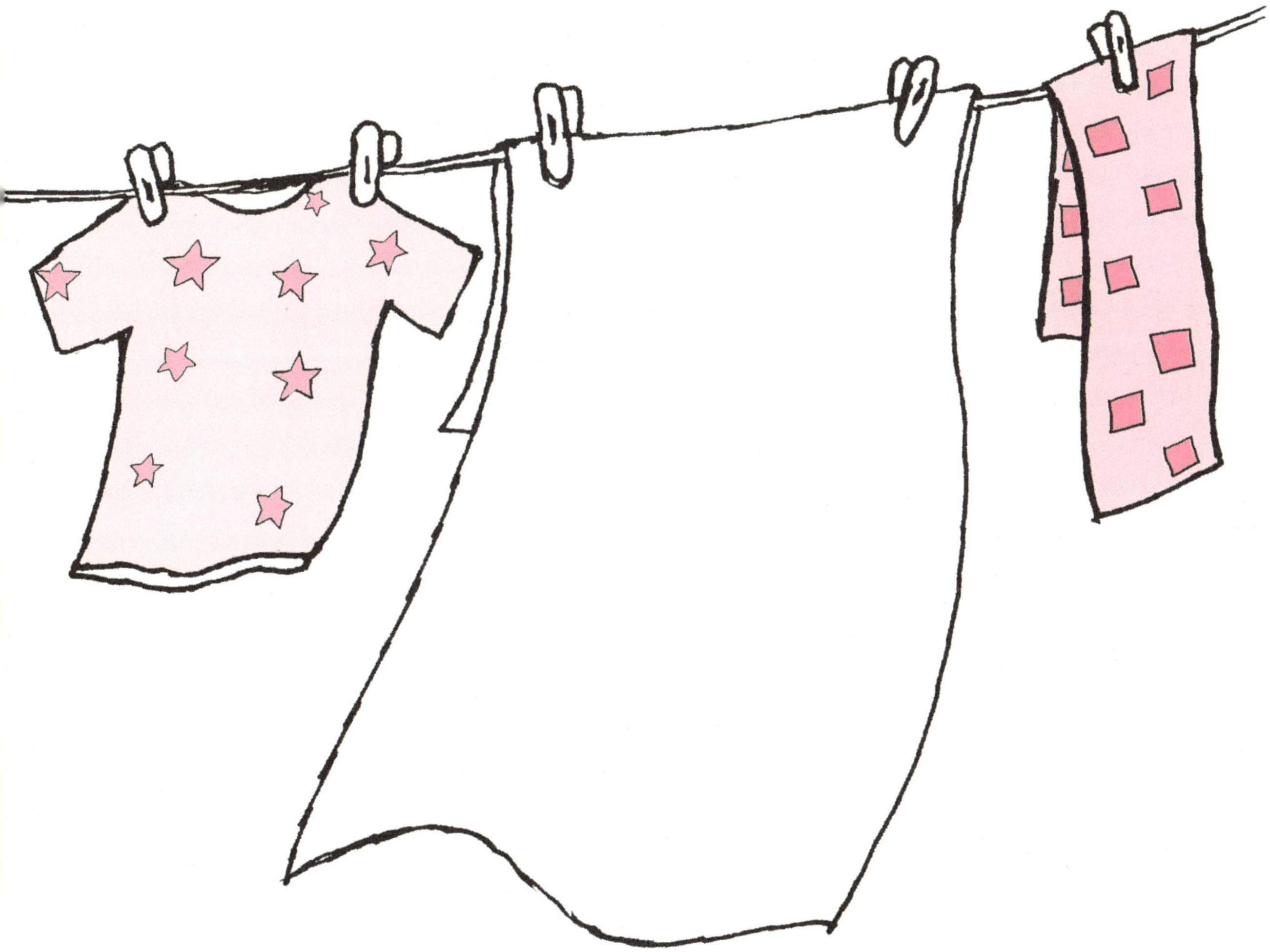

17 Decorating
Creative Cakes

■ Help me decorate the last cake.

To parents: If your child has difficulty, encourage him or her to look at the other cakes. He or she may want to copy some of the patterns shown.

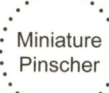

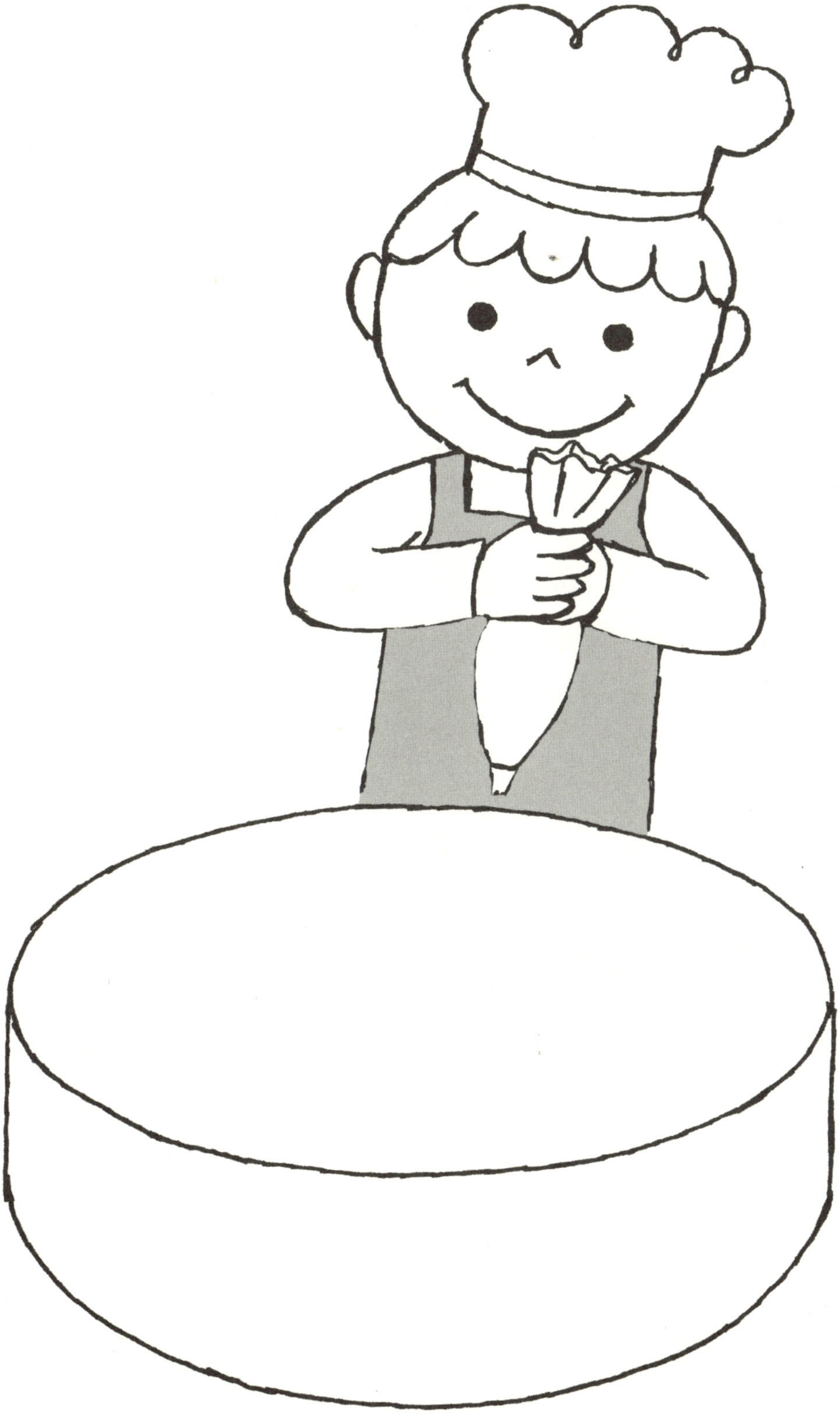

18 Decorating

Favorite Mugs

Decorate the two mugs.

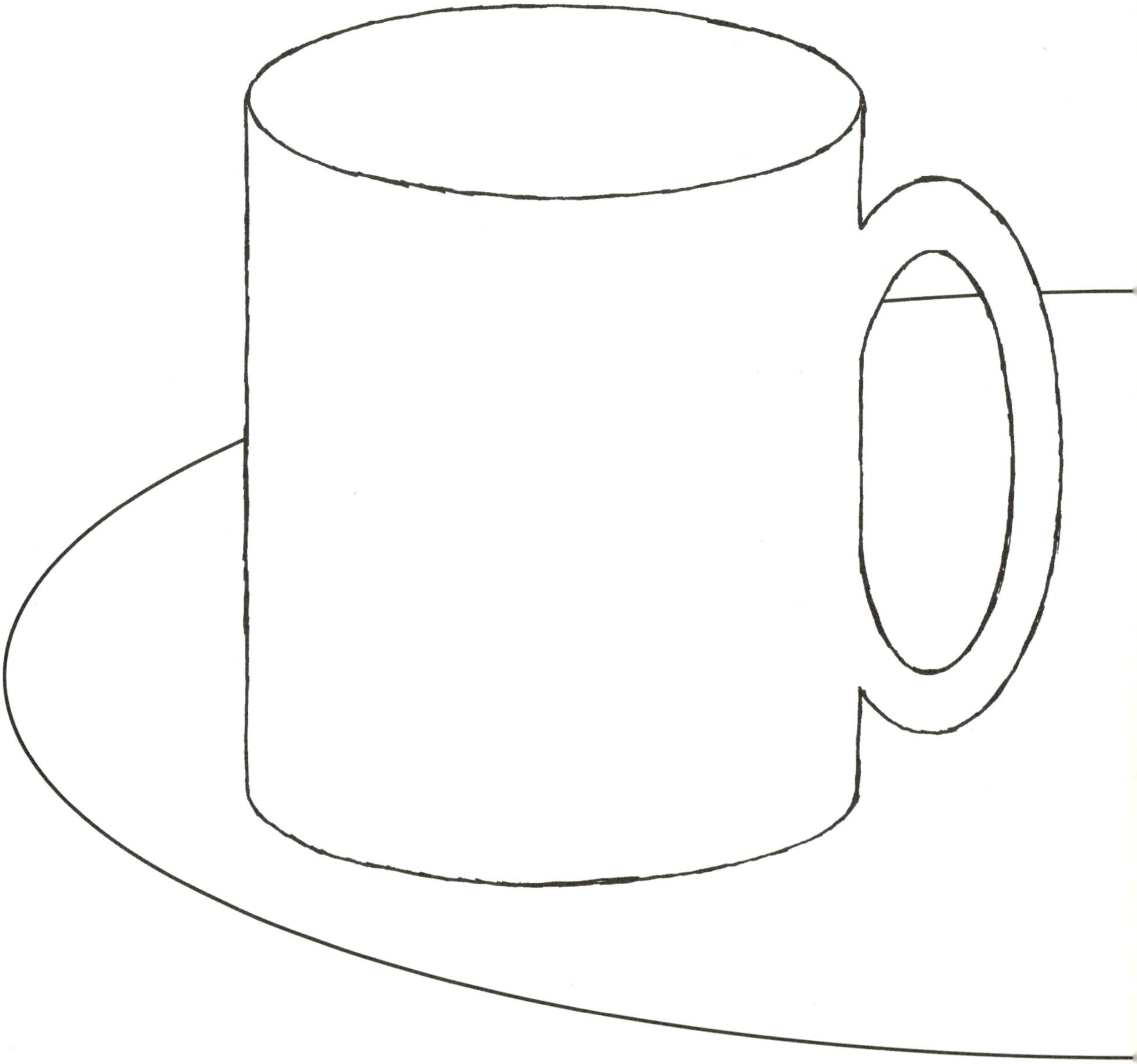

To parents: Starting with this activity, there are no patterns shown in the picture. This encourages your child to rely more on his or her own creativity.

Rough Collie

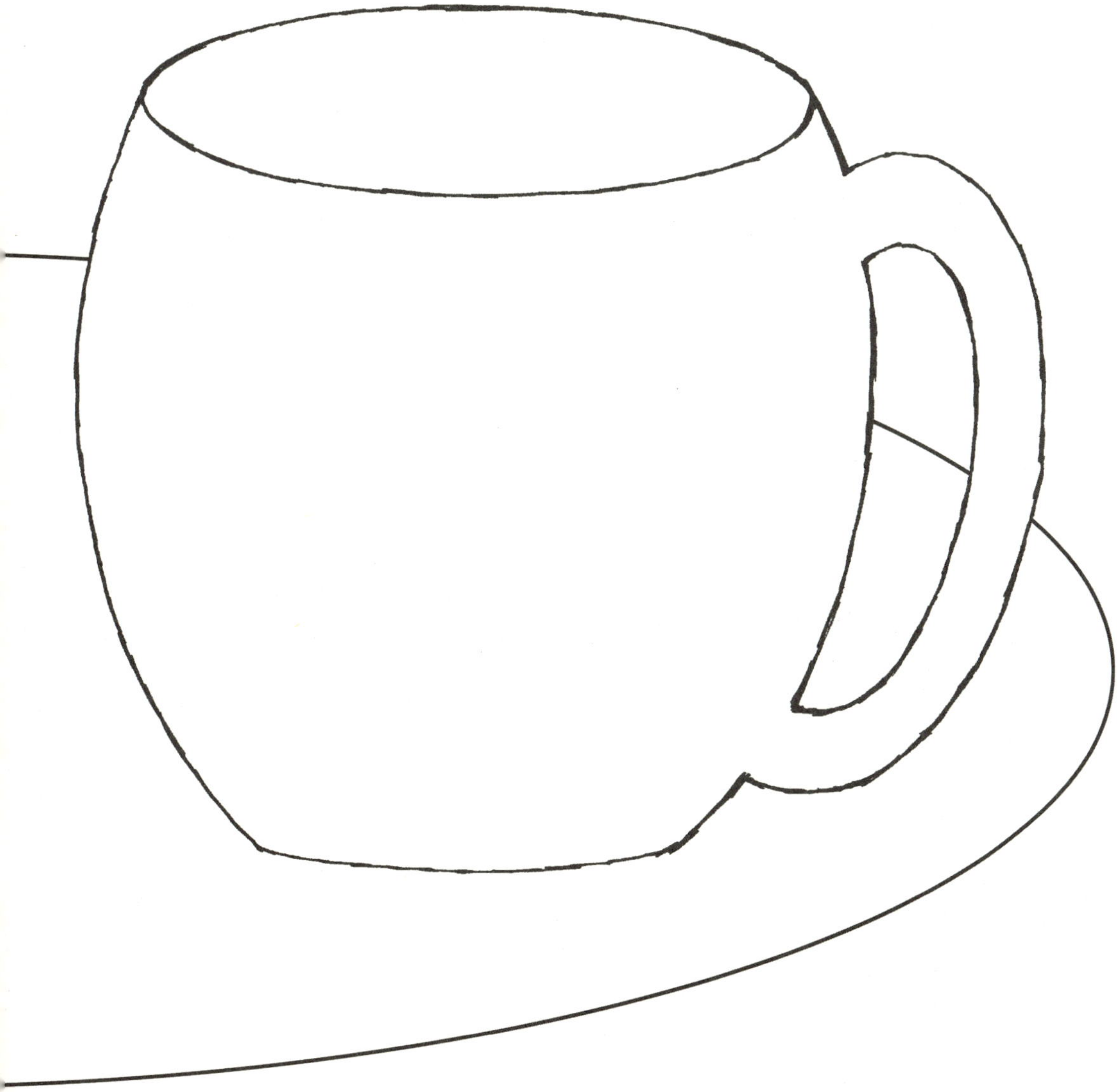

Decorating
Tropical Fish

■ Decorate the fish.

38

To parents: If your child has difficulty, you can review together some of the patterns in previous activities.

French Bulldog

20 Decorating
Awesome Cars

Decorate the cars.

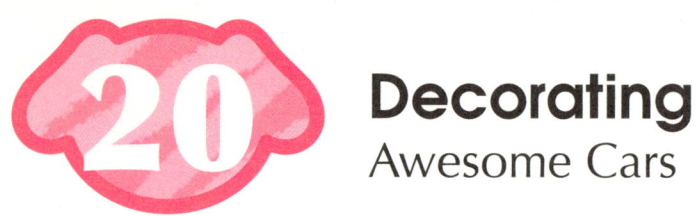

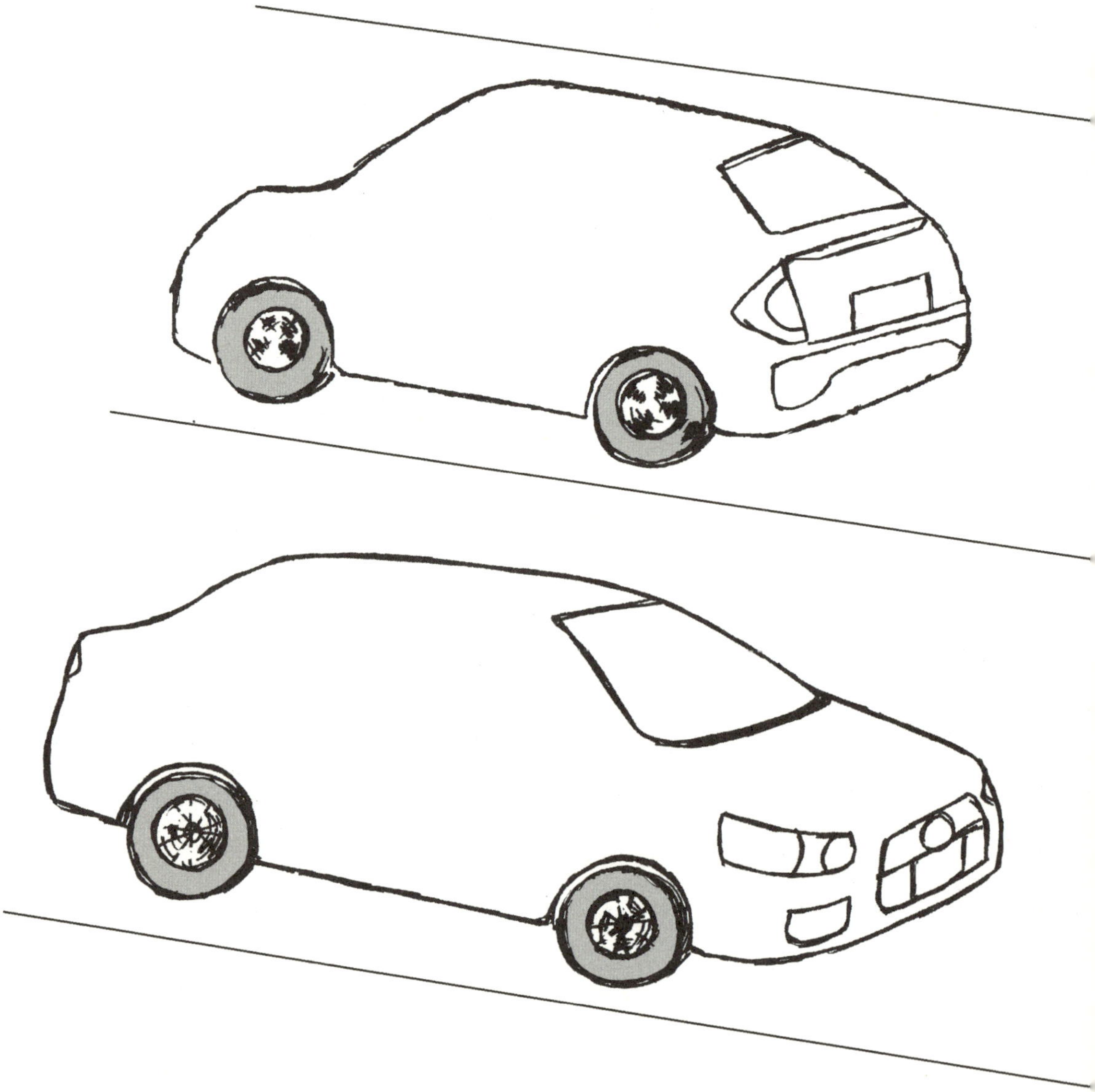

To parents: For a challenge, encourage your child to draw a different pattern on each of the four cars.

Papillon

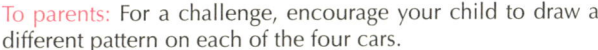

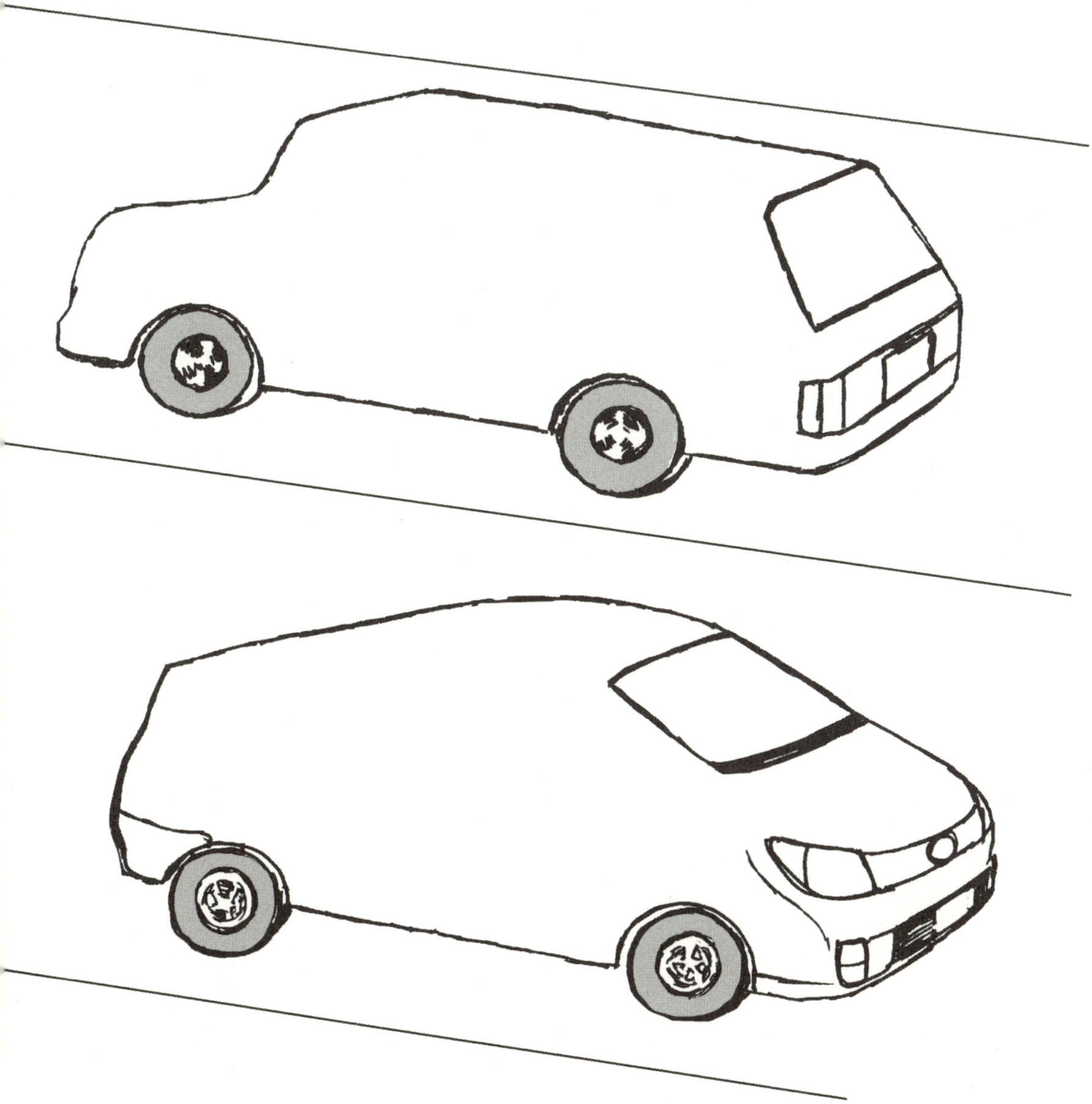

21 Drawing Something Specific
A Small Town

Draw more streets for the town.

To parents: Starting with this activity, your child will add something to the picture. The directions give specific information about what to add.

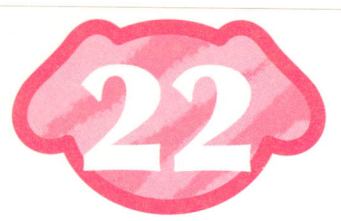

22 Drawing Something Specific
Blowing Bubbles

Draw more bubbles.

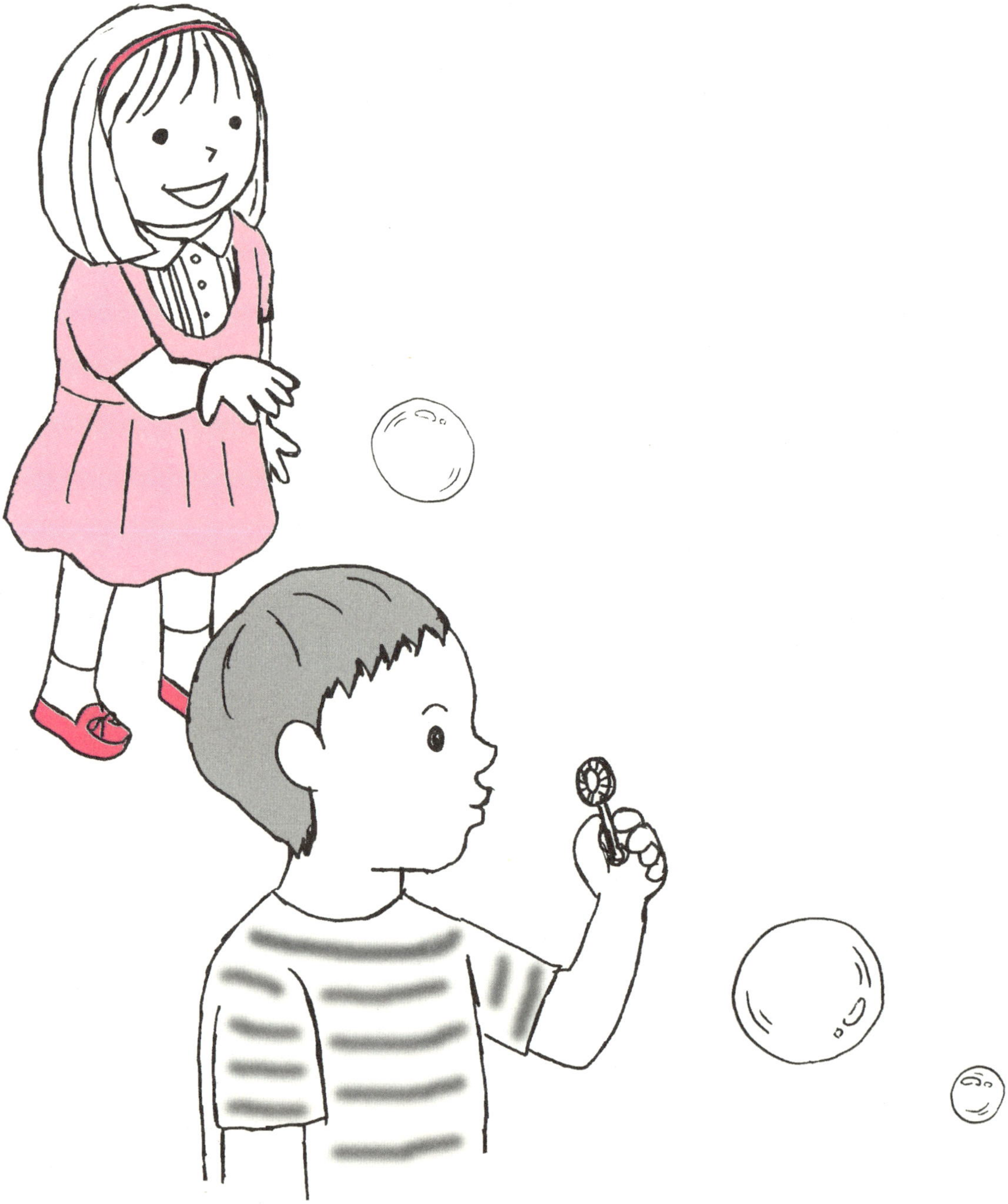

Bichon Frise

23 Drawing Something Specific

Catch the Balls

■ Help throw the balls.

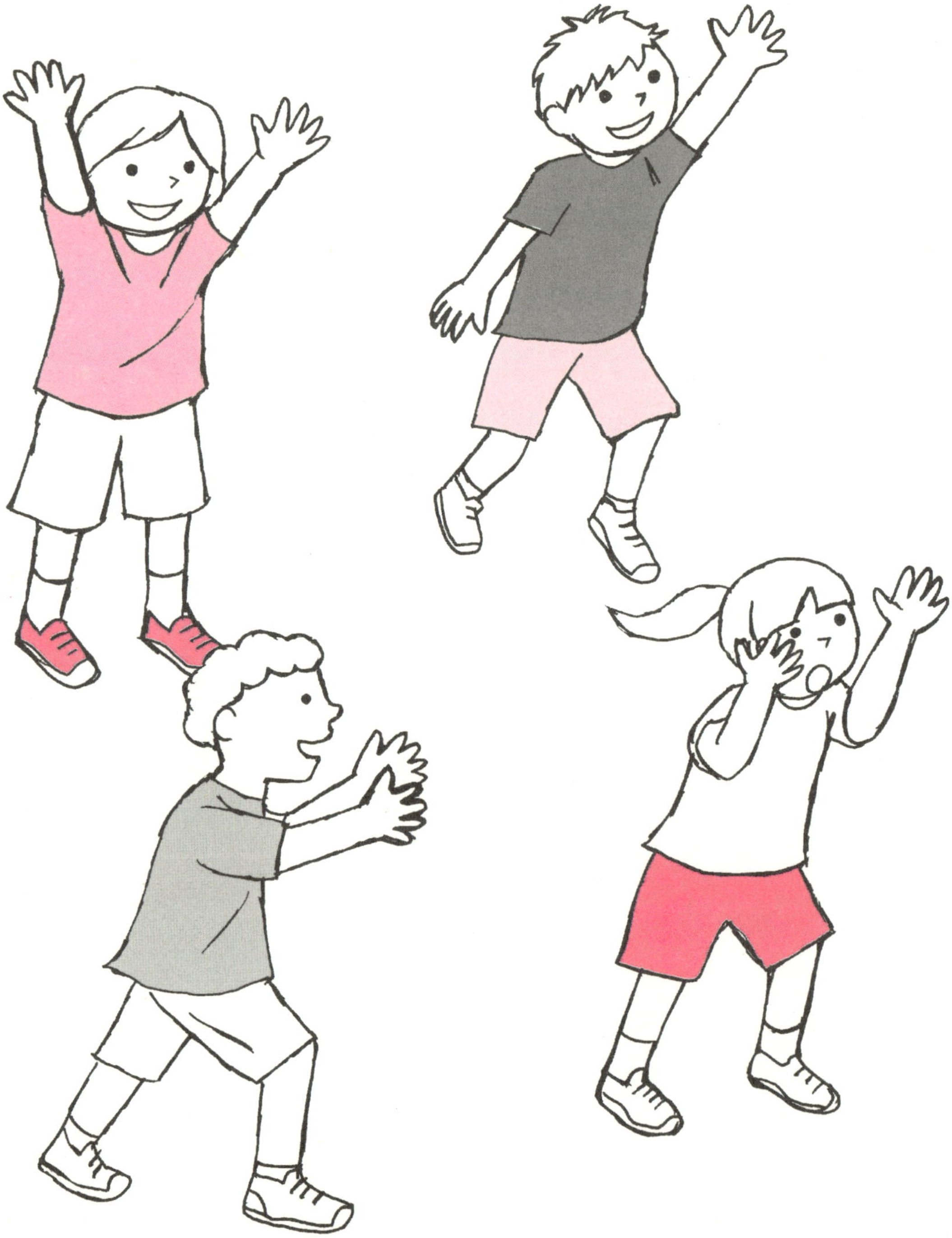

To parents: Your child can copy the balls shown in the picture or draw them in another way. Encourage your child to draw in the way that he or she feels most comfortable.

Border Collie

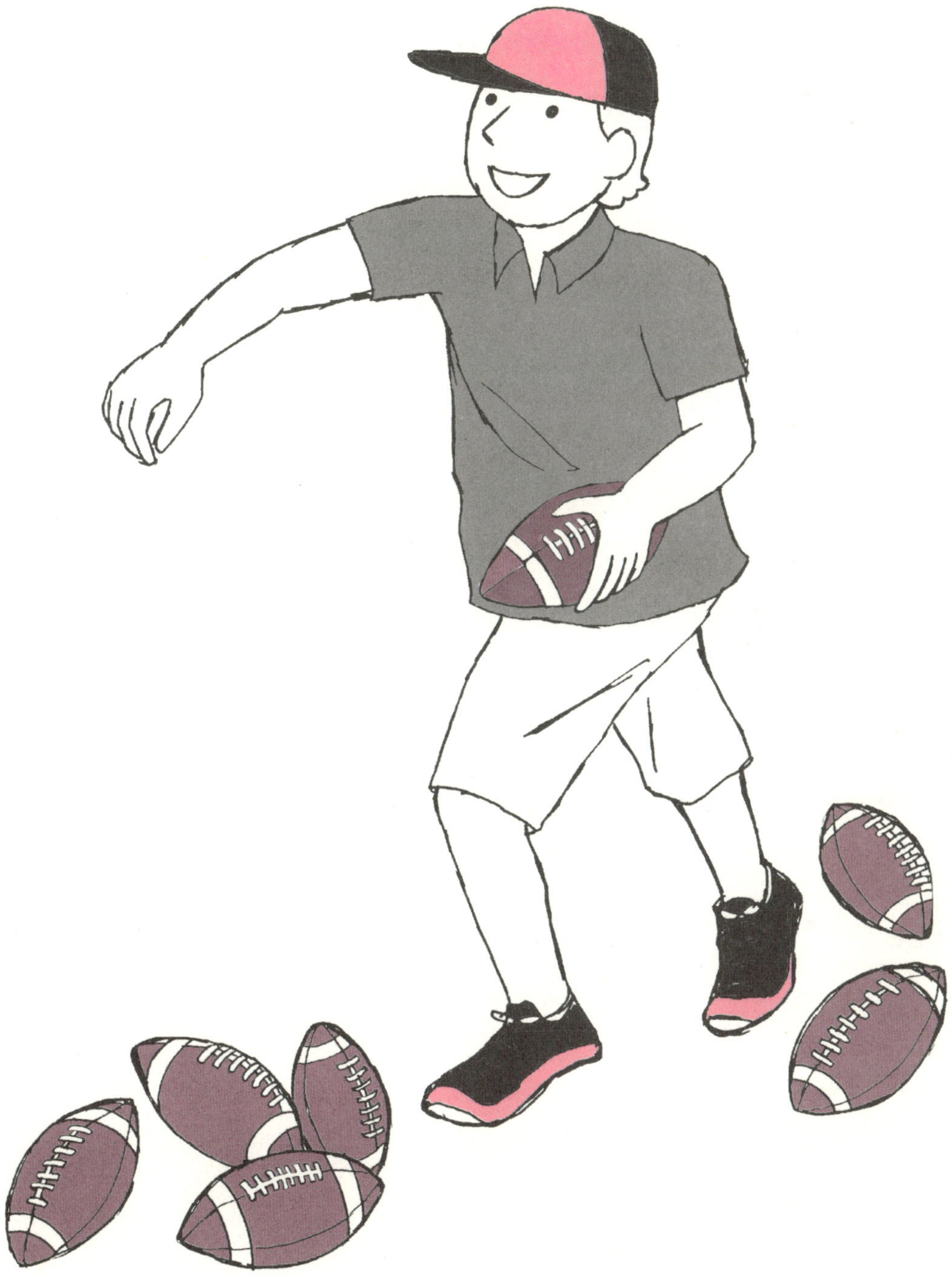

Drawing Something Specific
Under the Sea

■ Draw more fish.

Shetland
Sheepdog

25 Drawing Something Specific
Sand Castle Competition

Draw a winning sand castle.

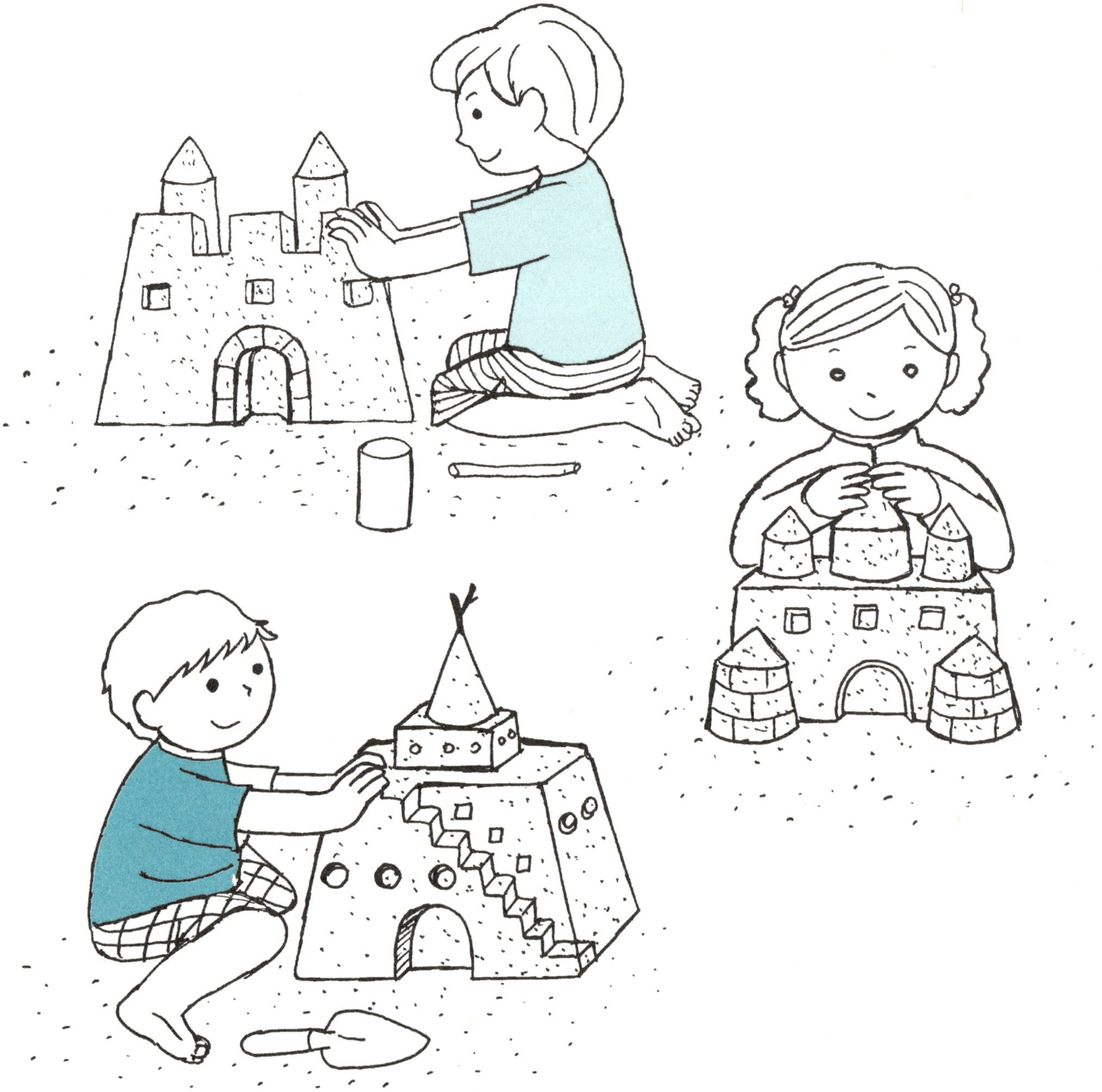

To parents: Starting with this activity, the picture shows a greater variety of examples of what to draw. If your child has difficulty, have your child choose one of the examples and try to copy it.

Boston
Terrier

26

Drawing Something Specific
In the Refrigerator

■ What is in the refrigerator?

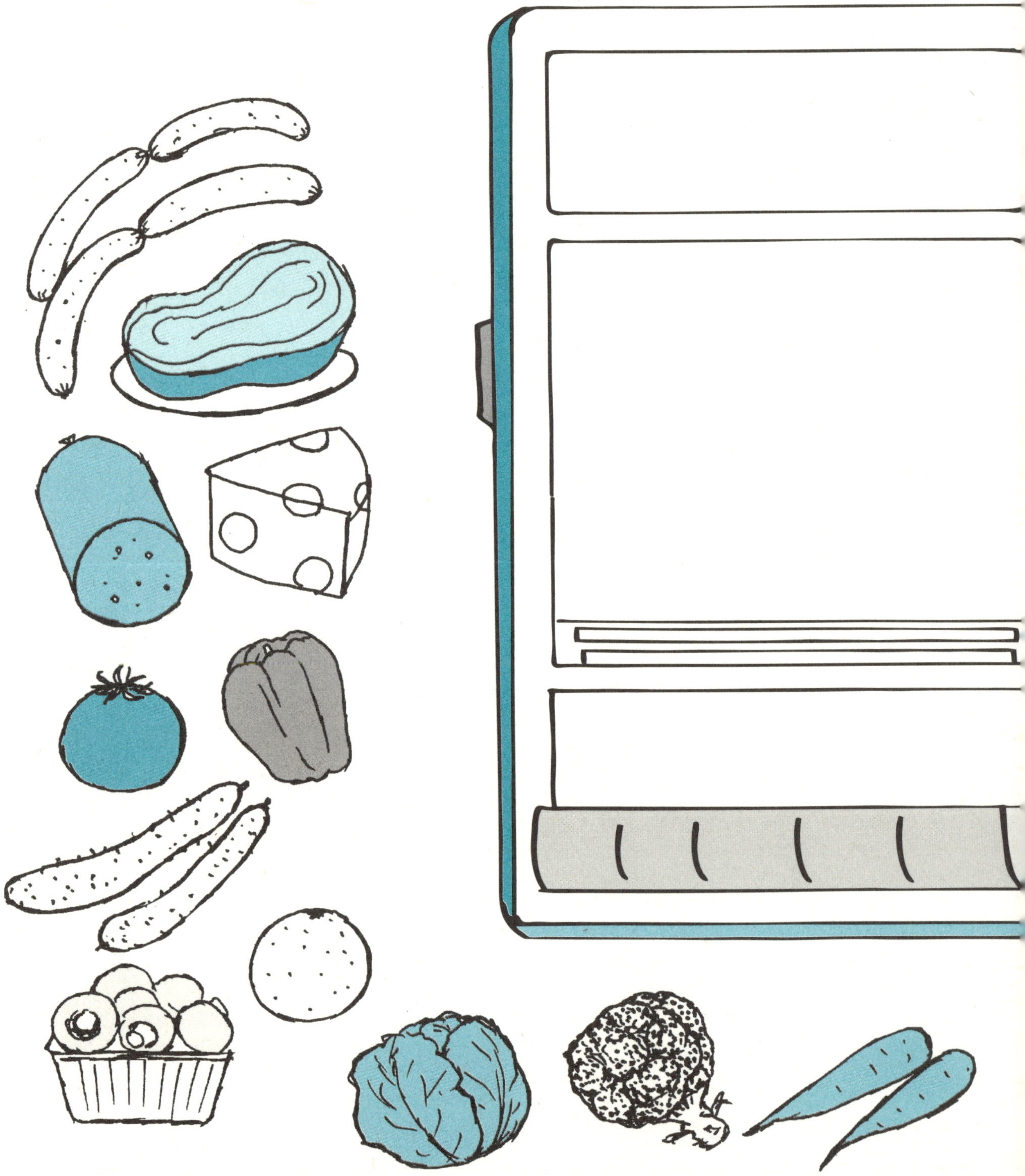

To parents: Your child can draw as many foods in the refrigerator as he or she would like.

Italian
Greyhound

27 Drawing Something Specific
Tall Mountains

■ Can you draw tall mountains?

American
Cocker
Spaniel

Drawing Something Specific
Kick the Ball

■ Where's the soccer ball?

Bernese Mountain Dog

Drawing Something Specific
A Big Spout

Can you draw the whale's spout?

Dalmatian

Drawing Something Specific
A Treasure Map

Draw a path to the treasure.

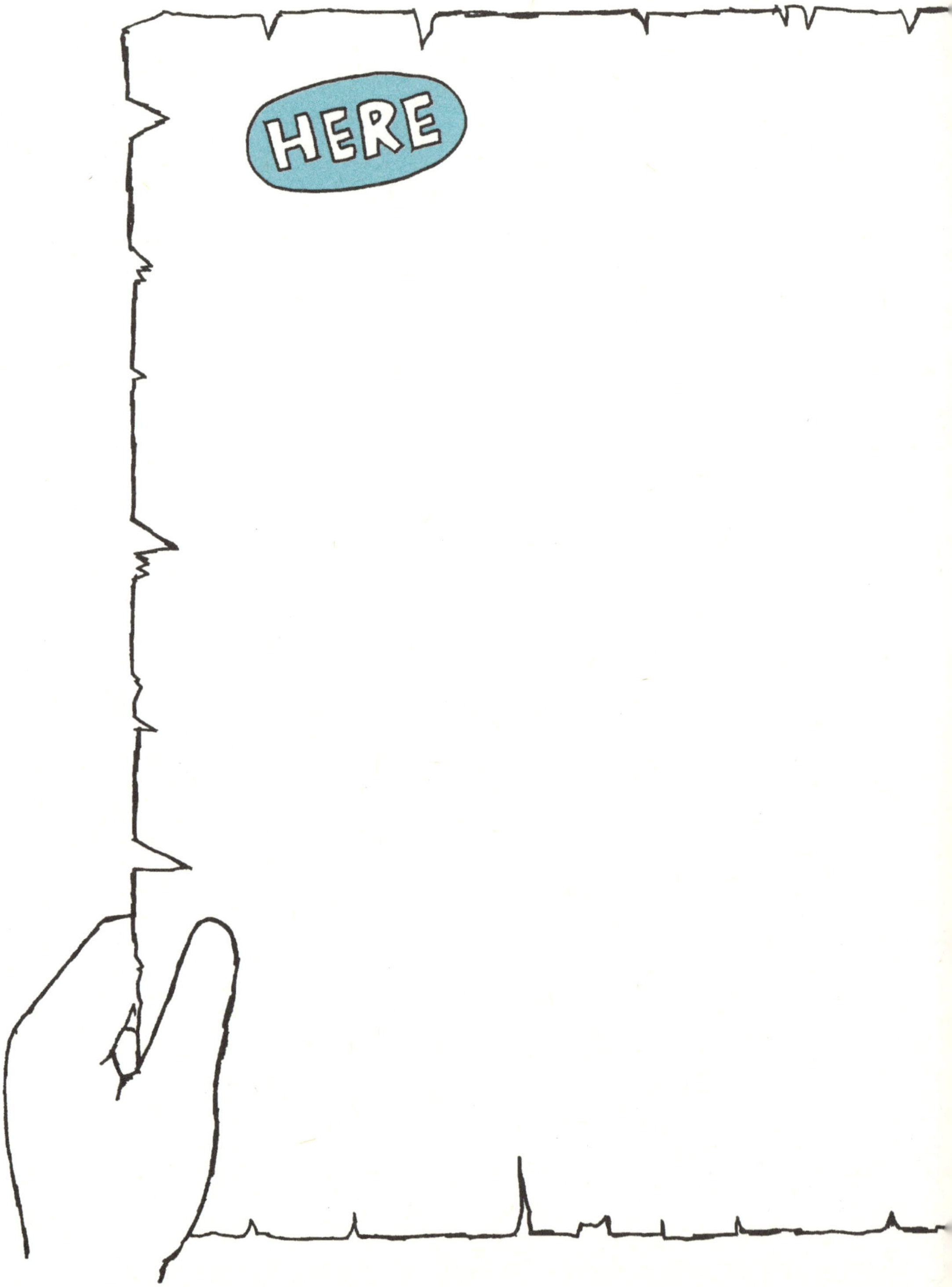

HERE

To parents: This is the last activity in this section. The
directions provide specific instructions about what to draw,
but they also leave a lot of room for creativity. Encourage
your child to have fun.

Drawing with Shapes
Time to Play

■ Turn these circles into a baseball and a soccer ball.

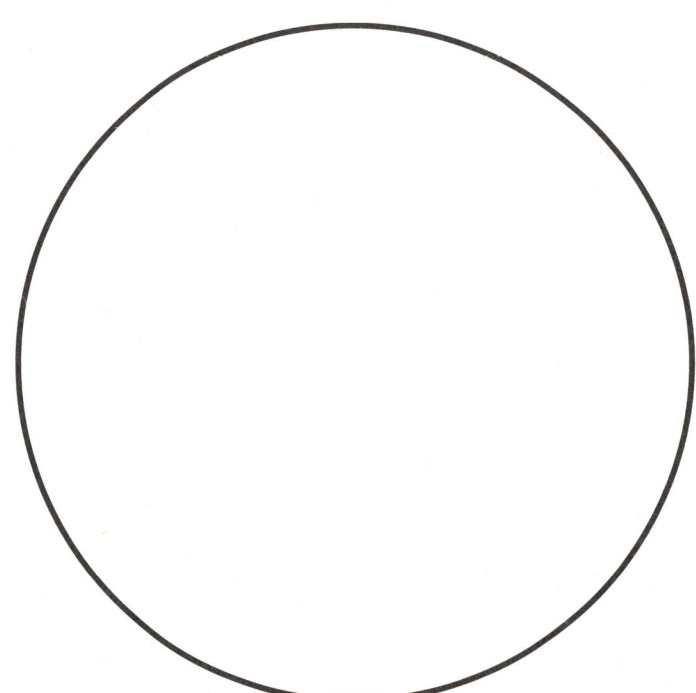

To parents: Starting with this activity, each page contains one or more shapes. The directions provide instructions about what to draw using the shapes.

Whippet

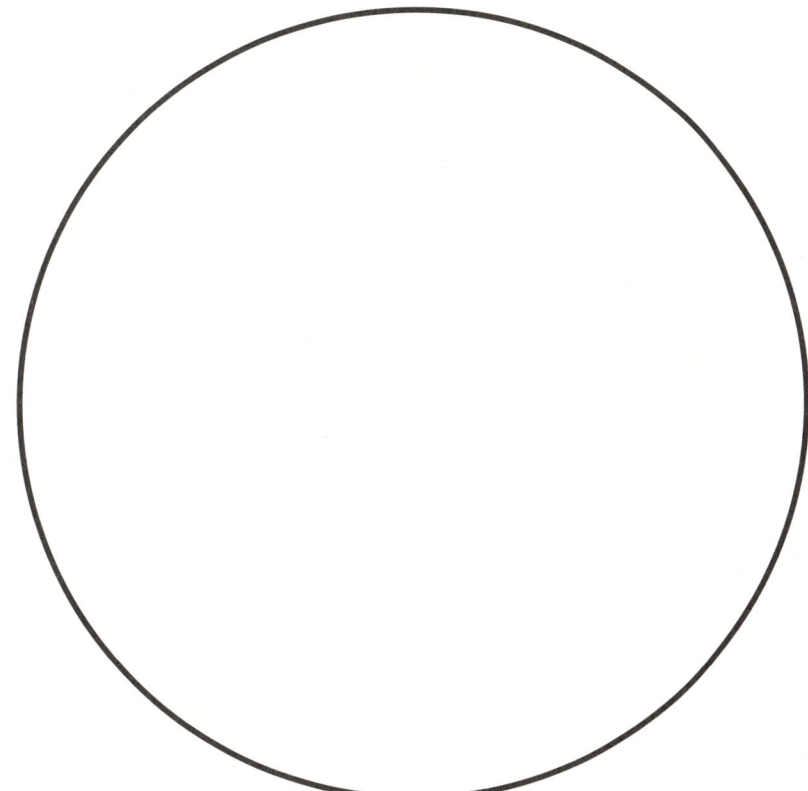

32

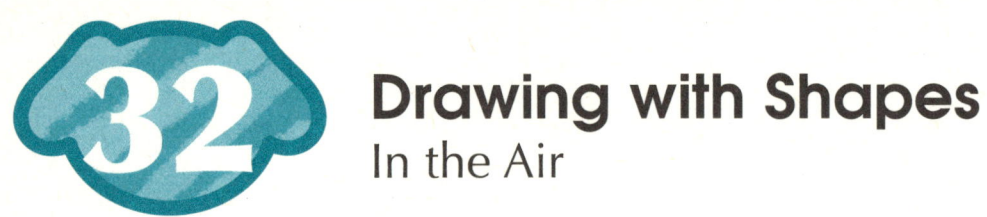

Drawing with Shapes
In the Air

Turn this shape into an airplane.

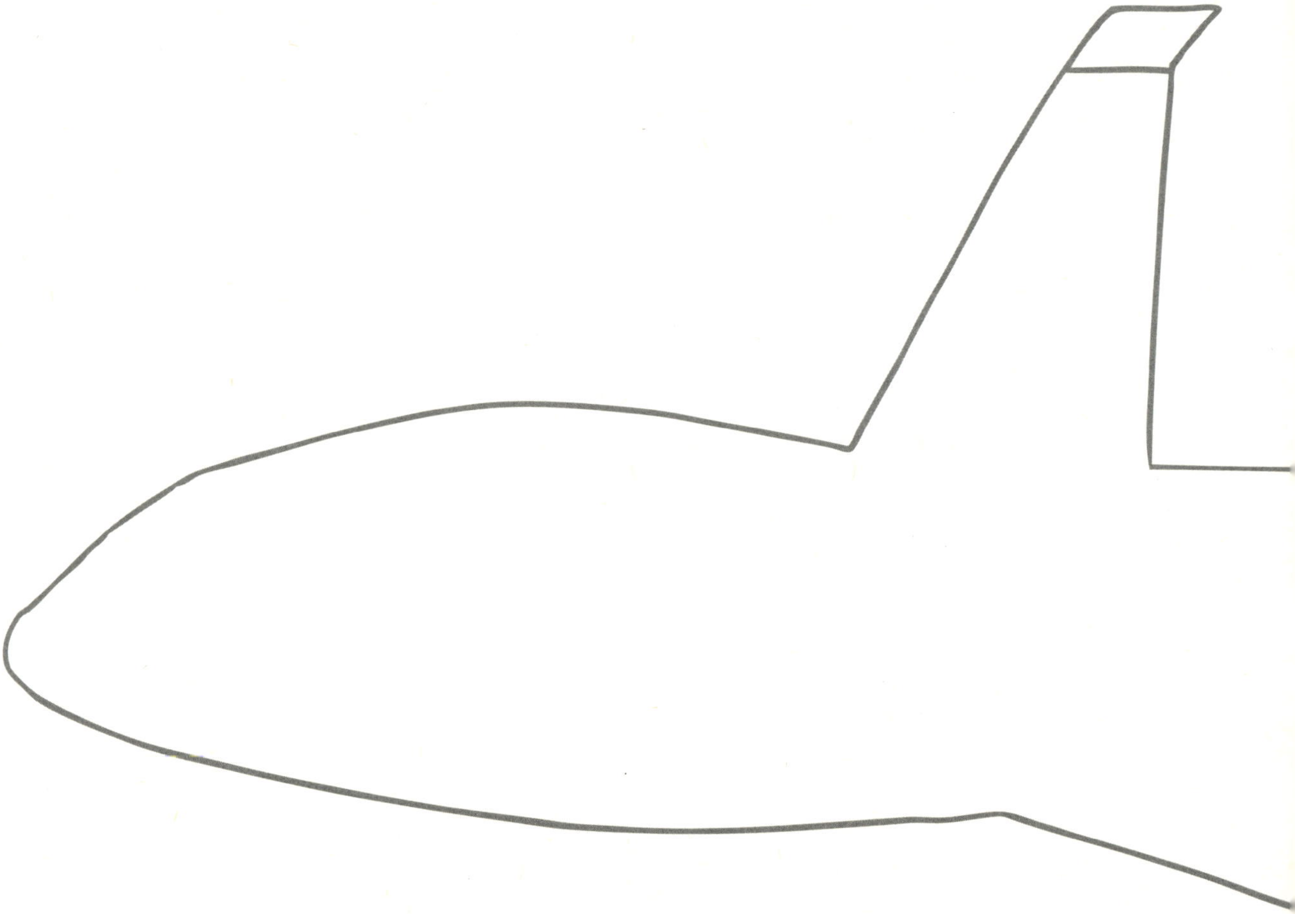

Kai

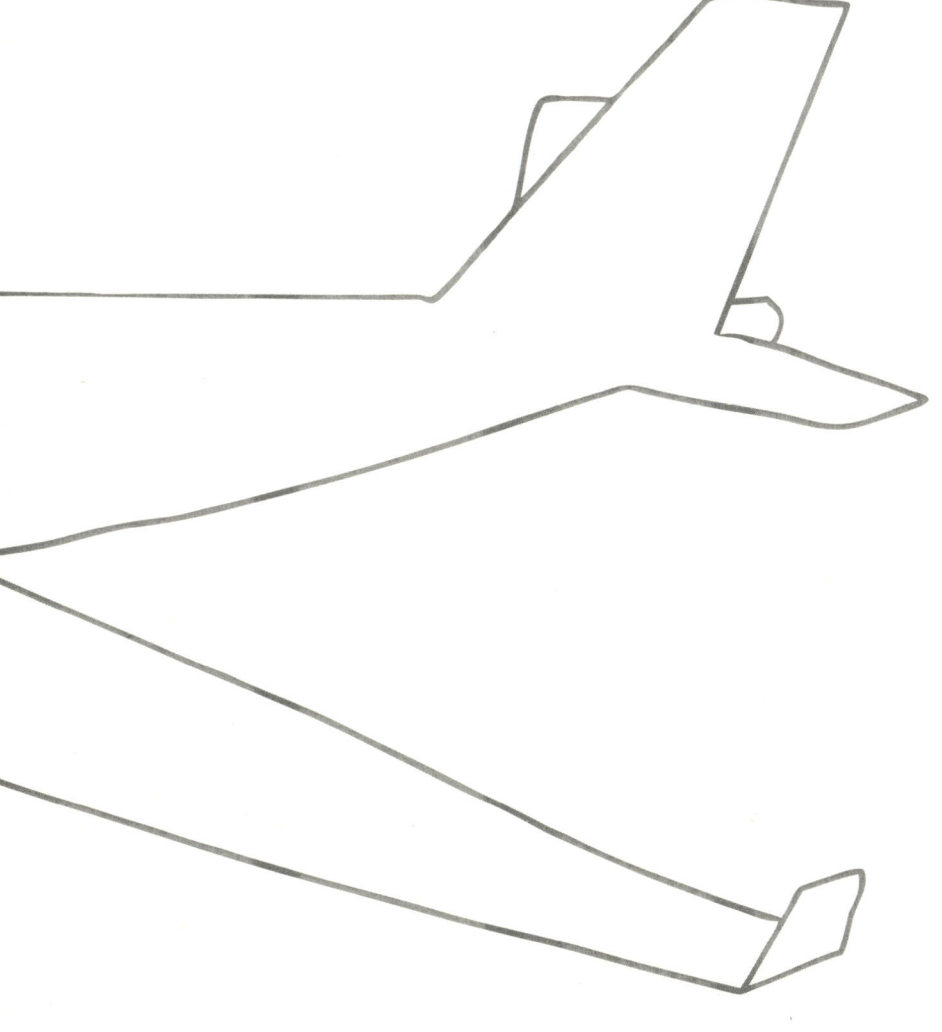

Drawing with Shapes
Pencils

■ Turn these shapes into pencils.

Basset
Hound

Turn these shapes into a banana and a strawberry.

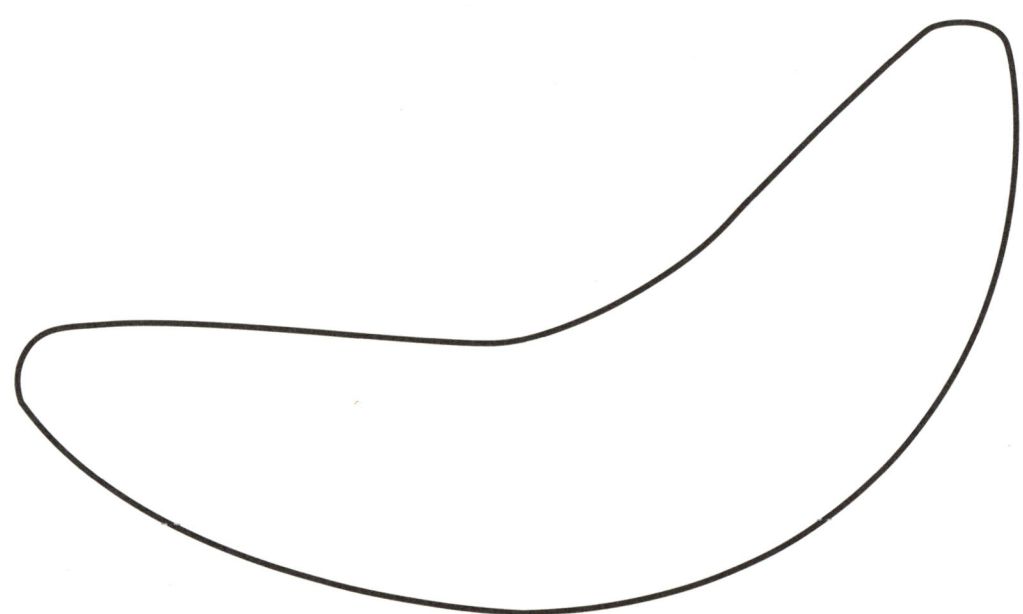

Siberian
Husky

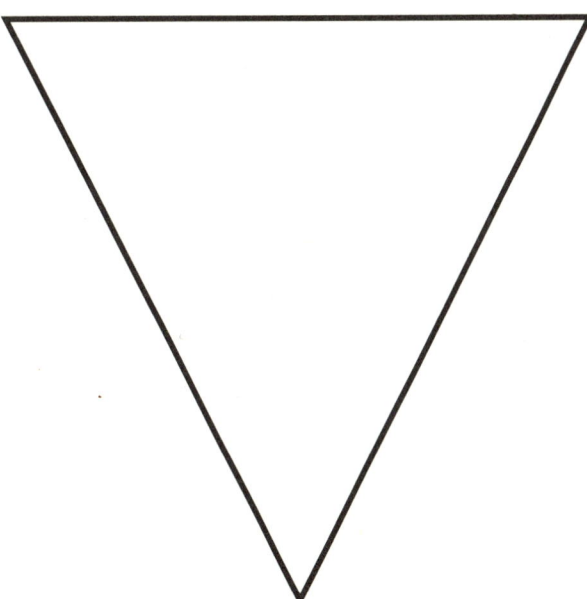

Drawing with Shapes
Happy Hedgehog

Turn this shape into a hedgehog.

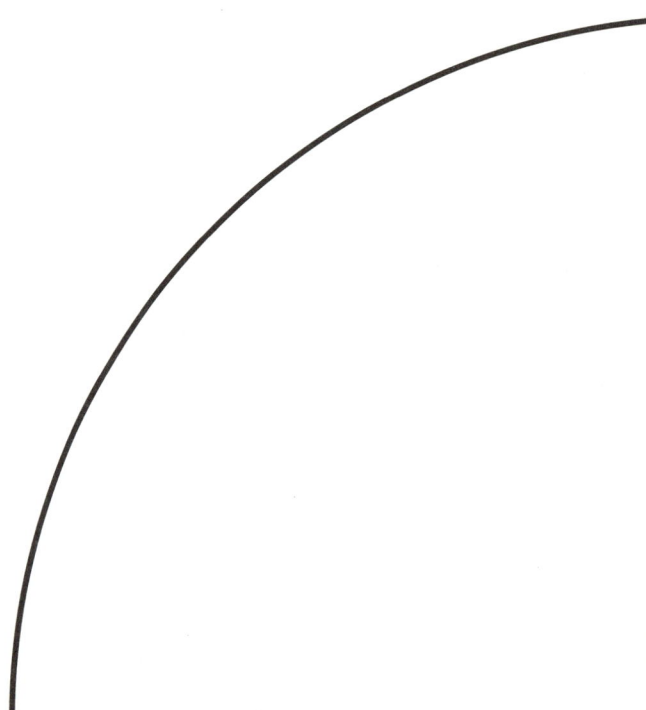

Basenji

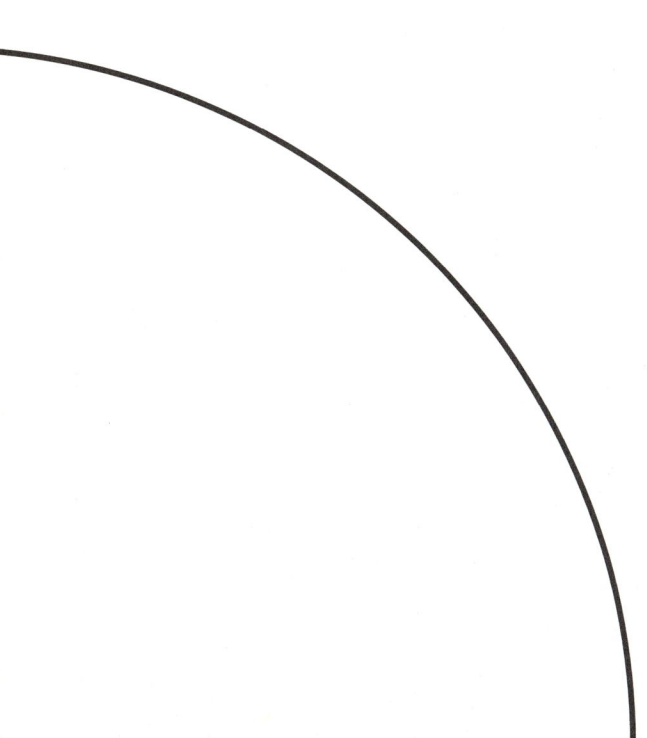

Drawing with Shapes
Brushing Teeth

■ Turn this shape into a toothbrush.

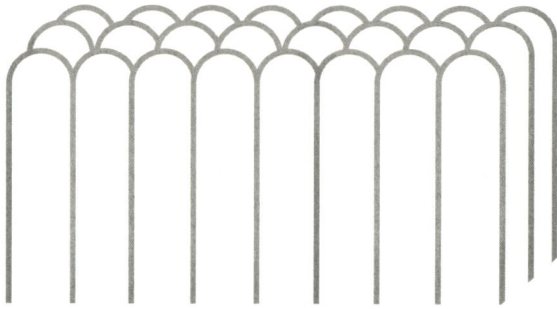

To parents: For an added challenge, encourage your child to think of a few different ways of creating his or her drawing, before getting started.

Doberman

Drawing with Shapes
Double Doors

■ Turn these shapes into doors.

Borzoi

Drawing with Shapes
Animal Ears

■ Turn these shapes into animal ears.

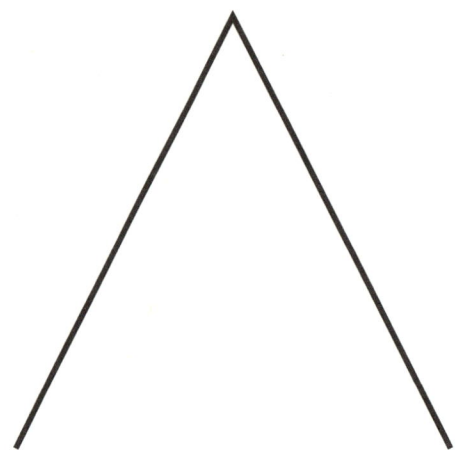

76

Rottweiler

Drawing with Shapes
Trapezoid

■ Turn these shapes into anything you want.

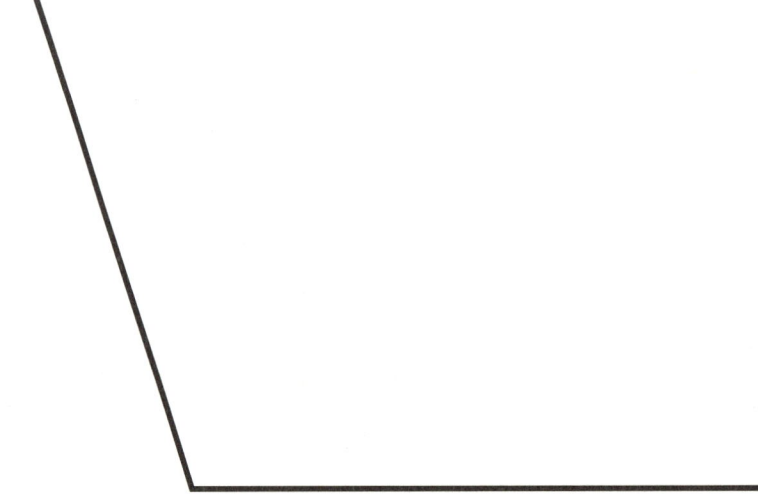

German
Shepherd

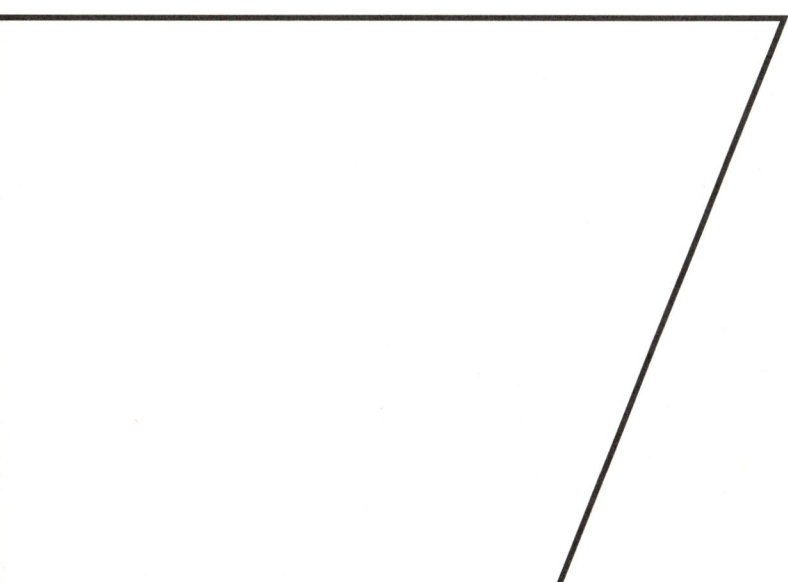

Drawing with Shapes
Two Blocks

■ Turn these shapes into anything you want.

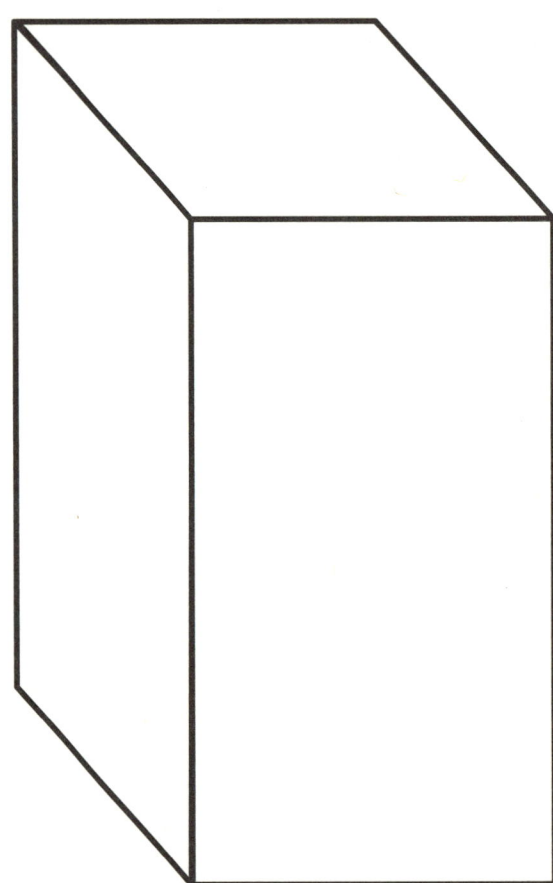

Great
Dane

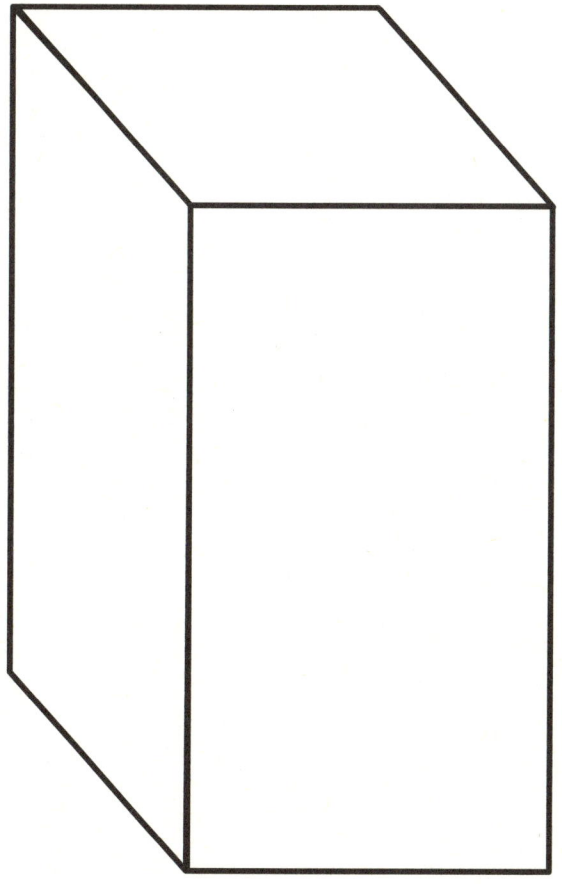

Drawing Something Creative
Time to Eat

■ What's cooking?

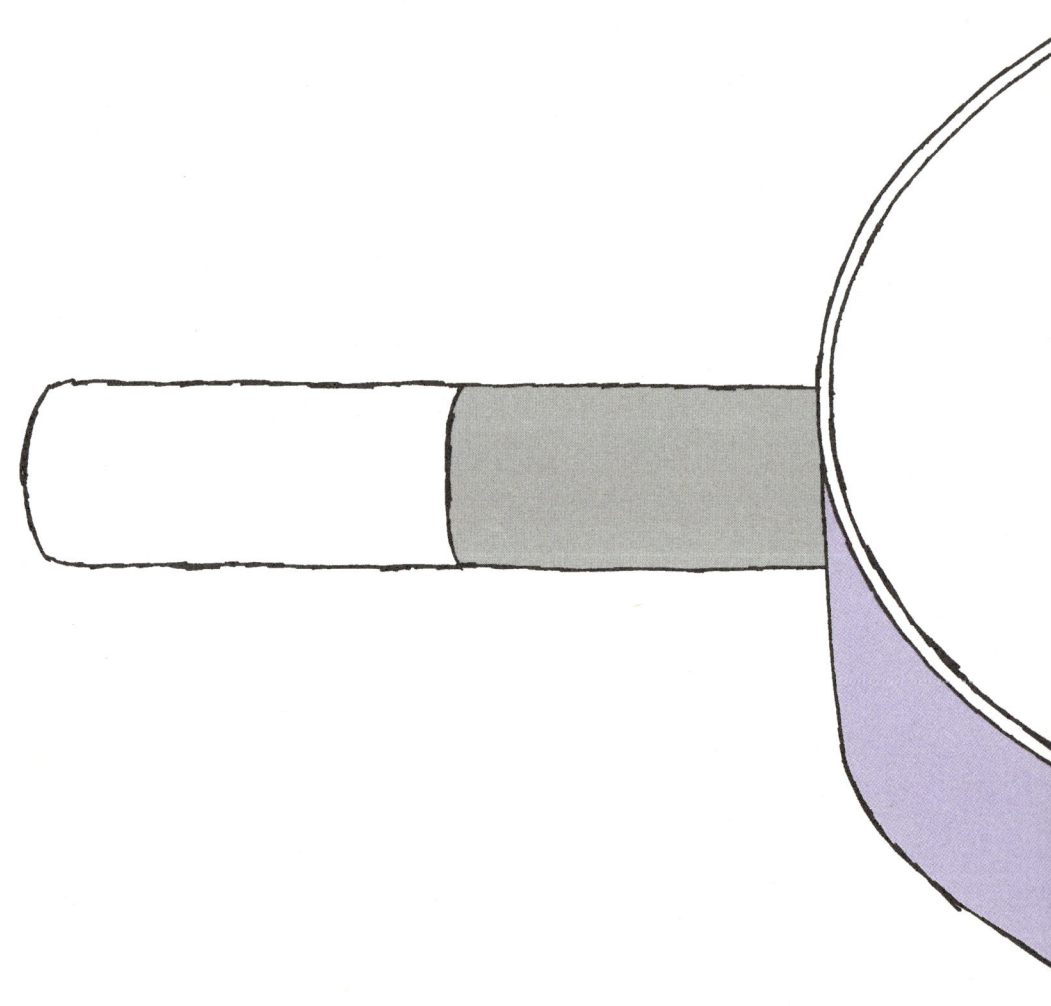

To parents: In this group of activities, your child will exercise creativity in deciding what to draw. Remind your child that there is no single correct response.

Boxer

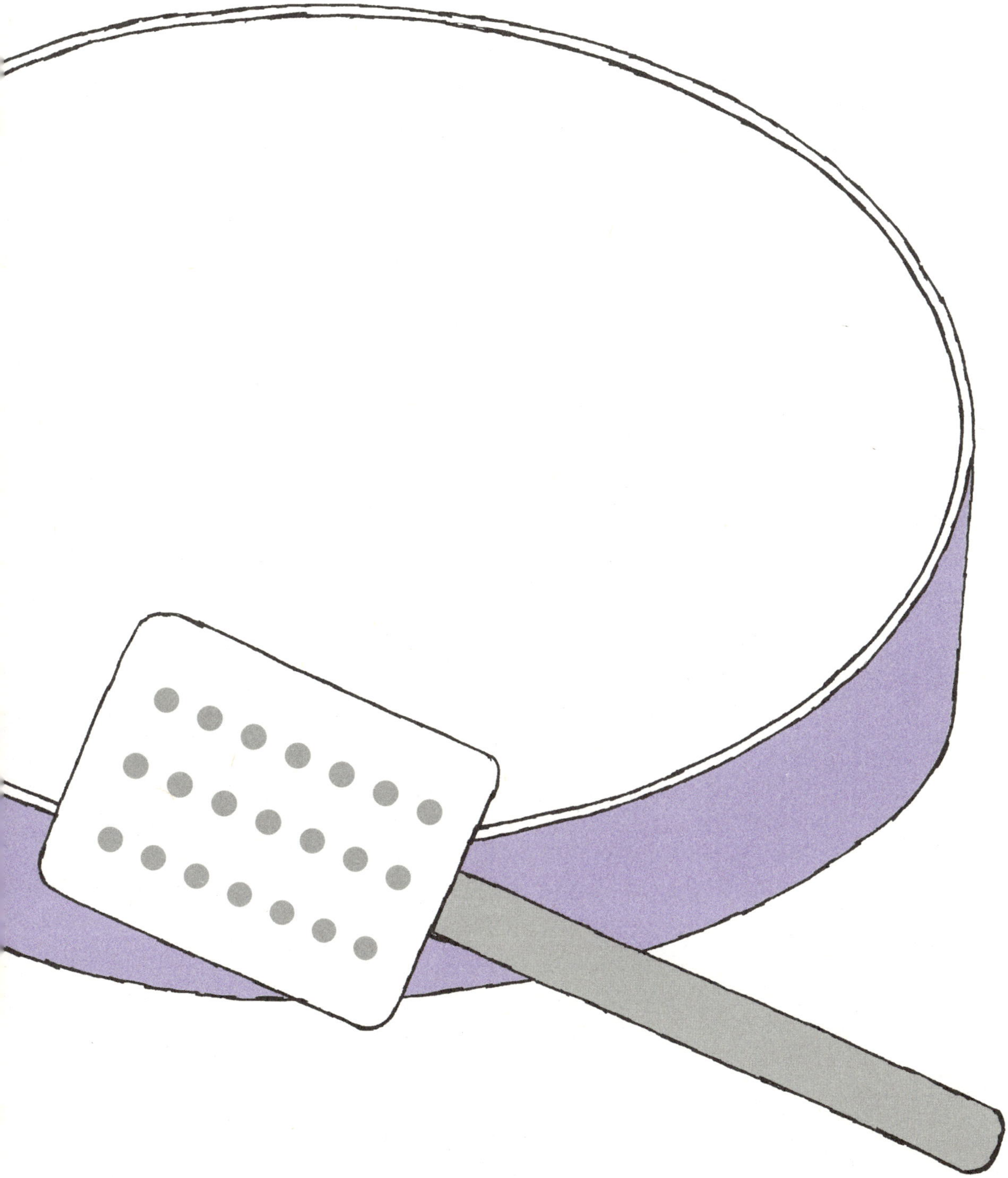

42 Drawing Something Creative

A Treasure Chest

What's in the treasure chest?

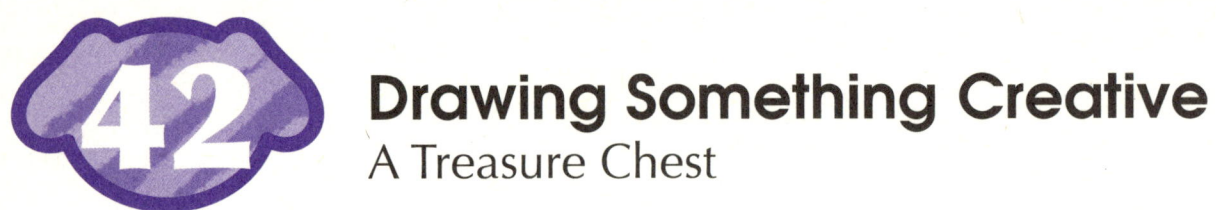

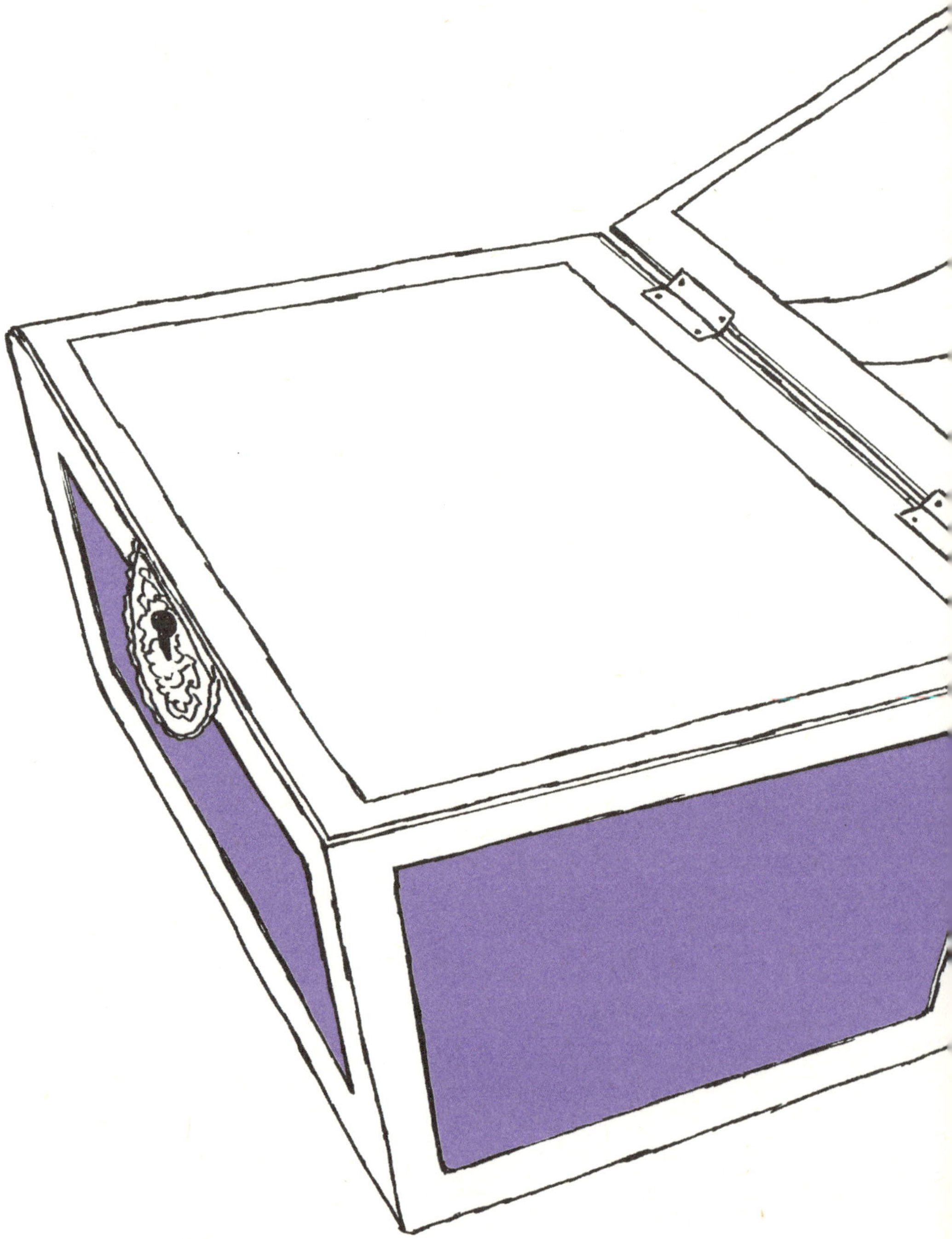

English
Springer
Spaniel

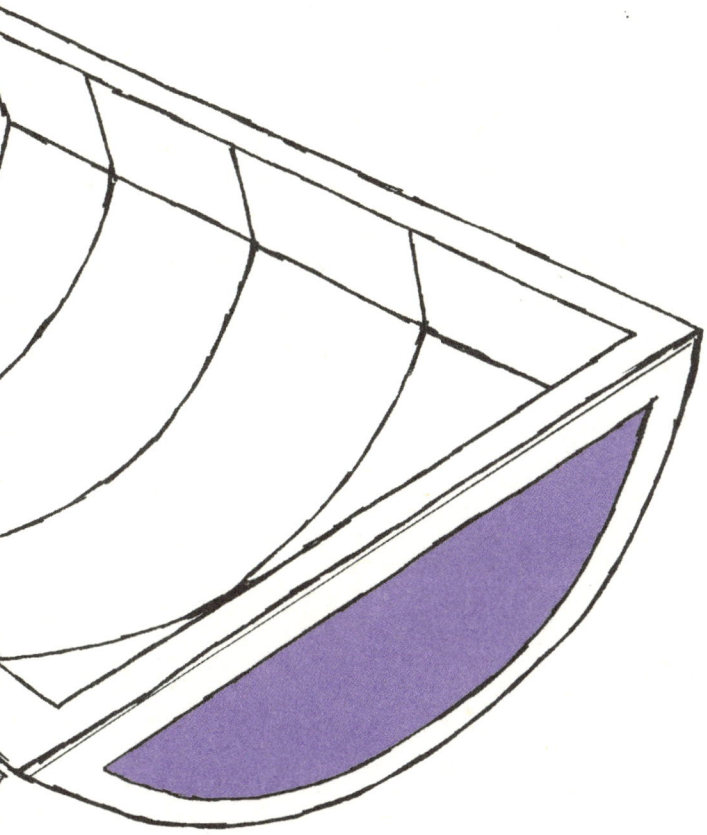

■ What did the bear catch?

Akita

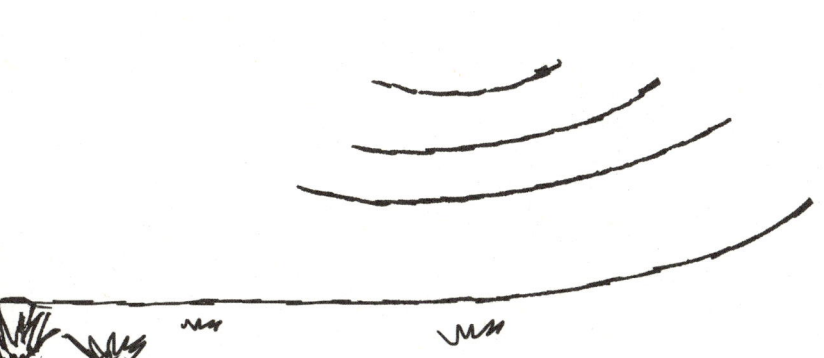

Akita

44

Drawing Something Creative

Down from the Mountain

Who or what is coming down from the mountain?

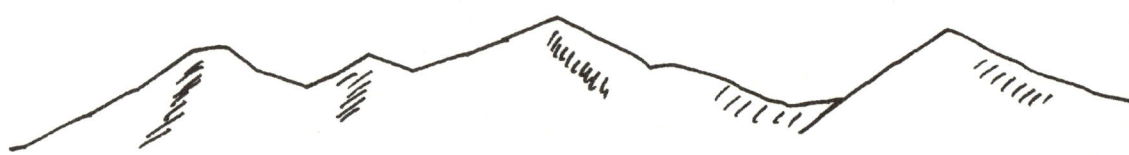

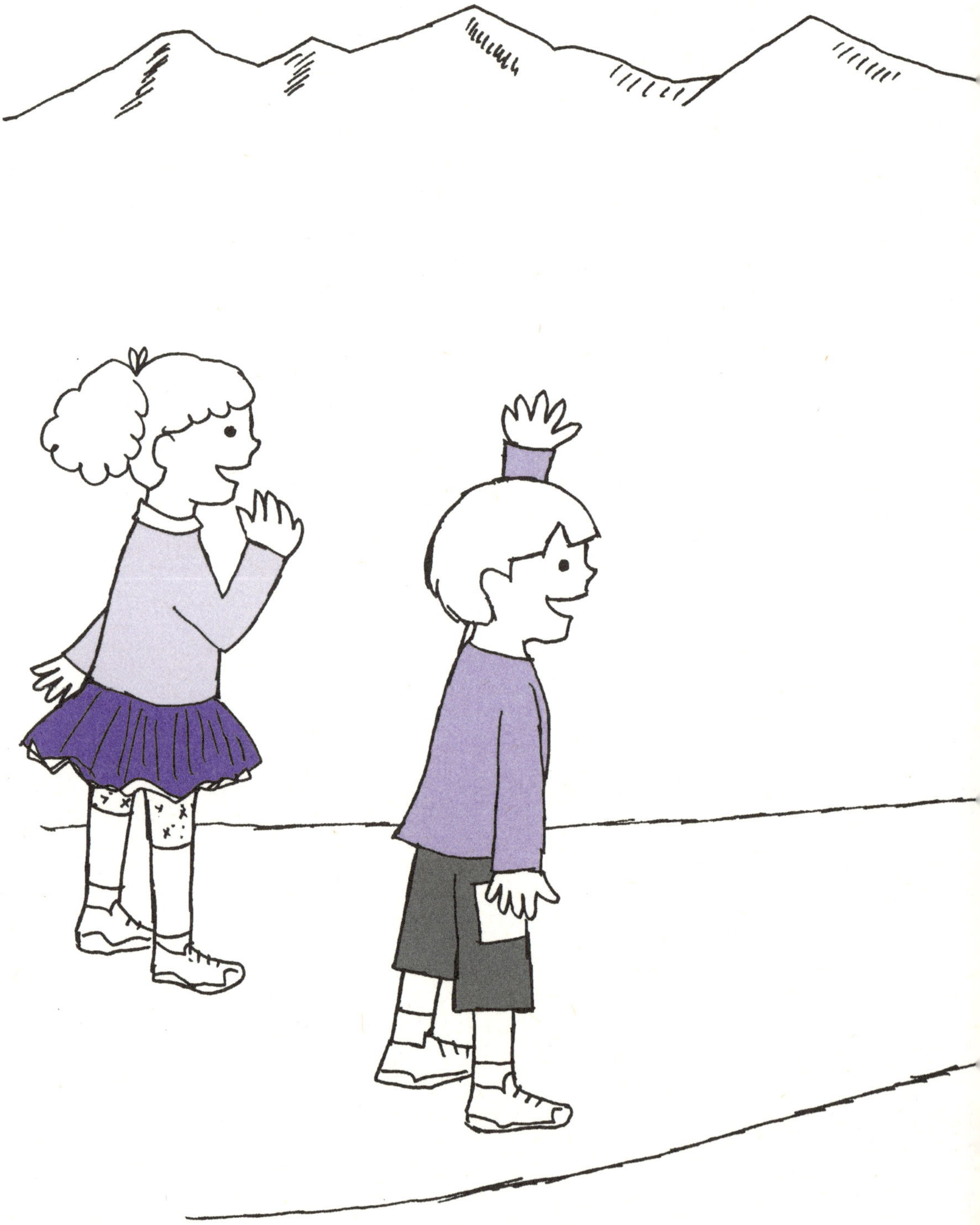

To parents: You may wish to encourage your child to plan out his or her drawing before getting started.

Border Terrier

45 Drawing Something Creative
Walking Through the Museum

■ Can you draw a picture in the blank painting?

To parents: You might want to encourage your child to draw his or her favorite things in the painting.

Brittany Spaniel

Drawing Something Creative
Strangely Shaped Rainbow

■ A strangely shaped rainbow appears in the sky. Can you draw it?

To parents: Remember that your child's drawing does not need to show something that can happen in real life.

Clumber
Spaniel

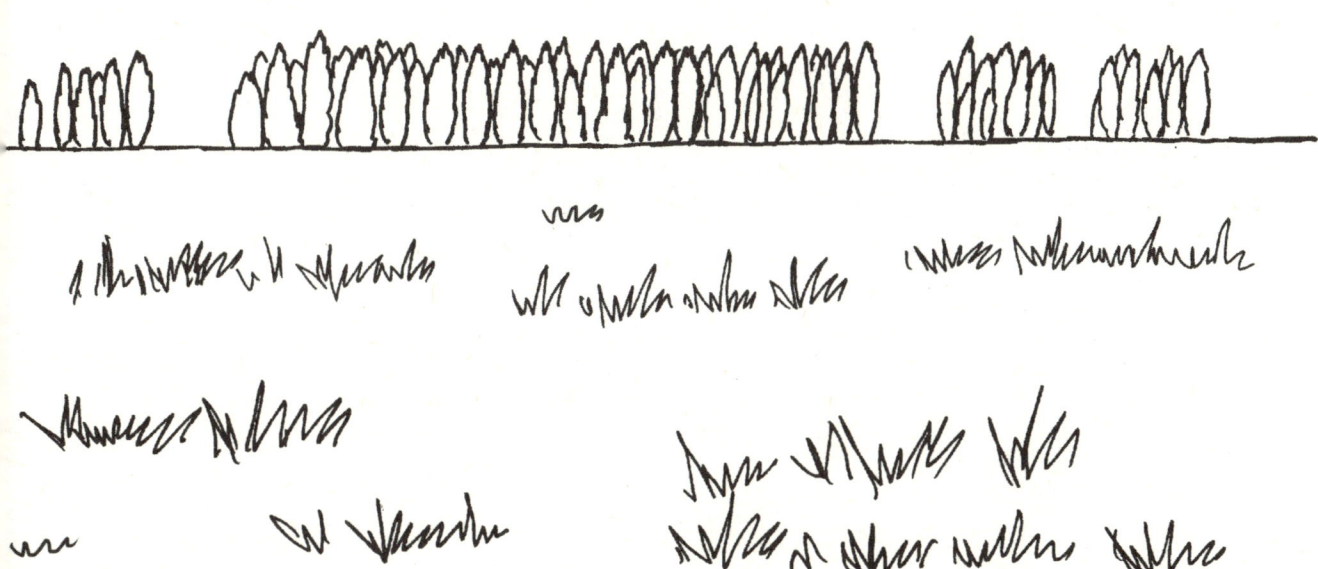

47

Drawing Something Creative

A Jungle Expedition

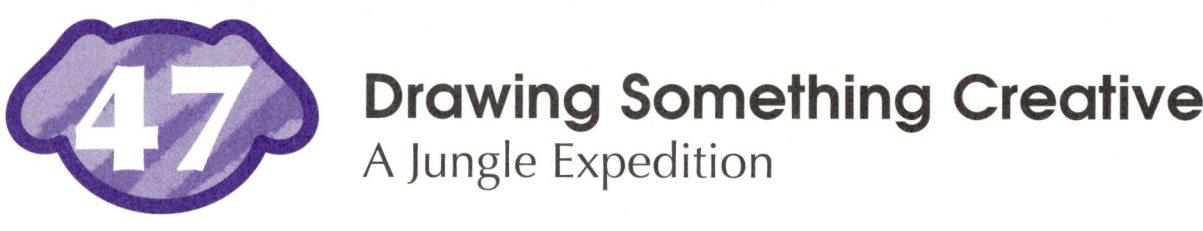

■ What do the explorers find in the jungle?

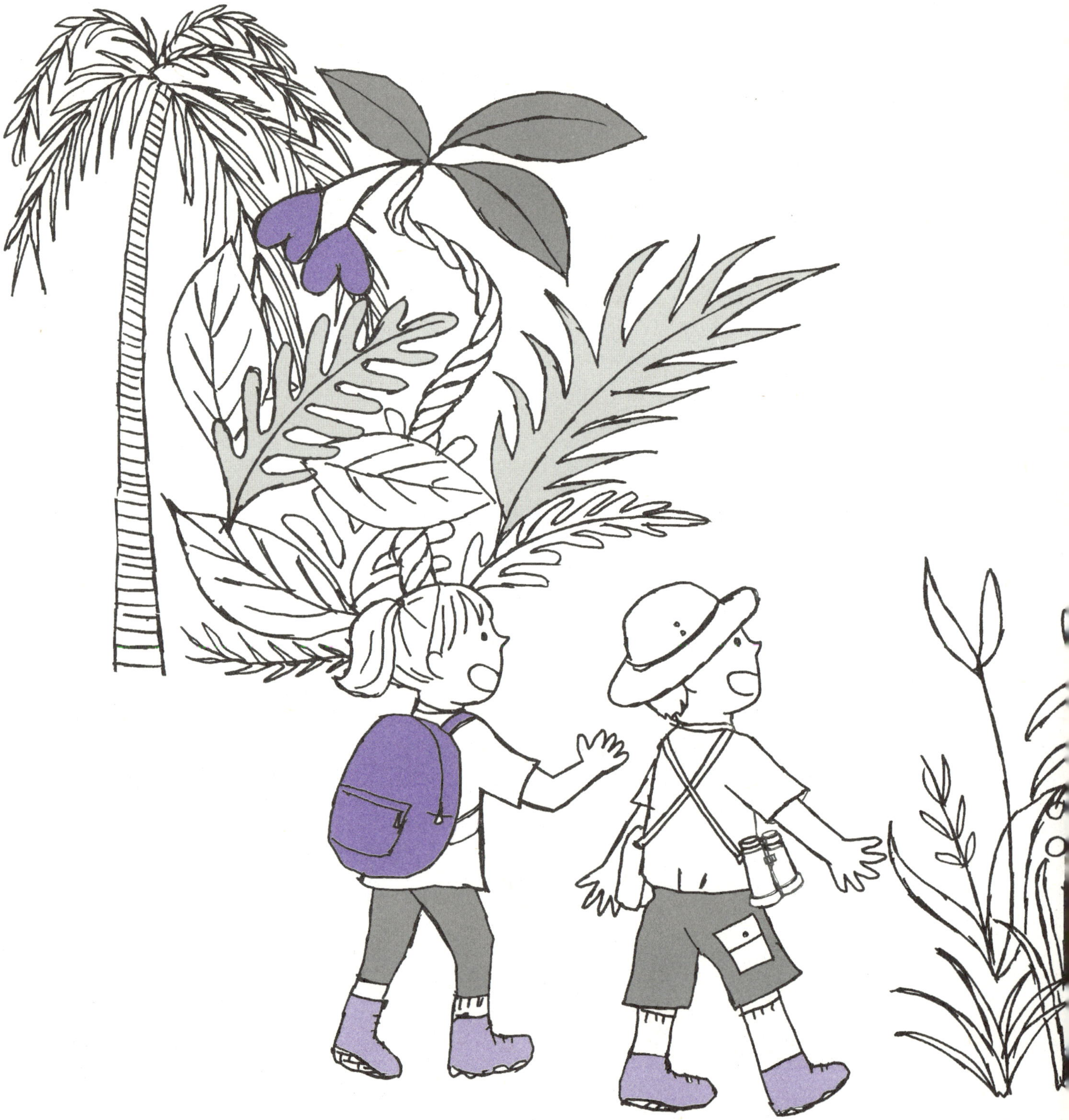

Belgian Shepherd

Drawing Something Creative
Undiscovered Island

■ Draw an undiscovered island.

To parents: If your child has difficulty, help your child brainstorm ideas or refer to page 128.

English Setter

■ What do the explorers find underground?

To parents: Encourage your child to talk about what he or she wants to draw, before getting started.

Japanese Chin

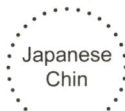

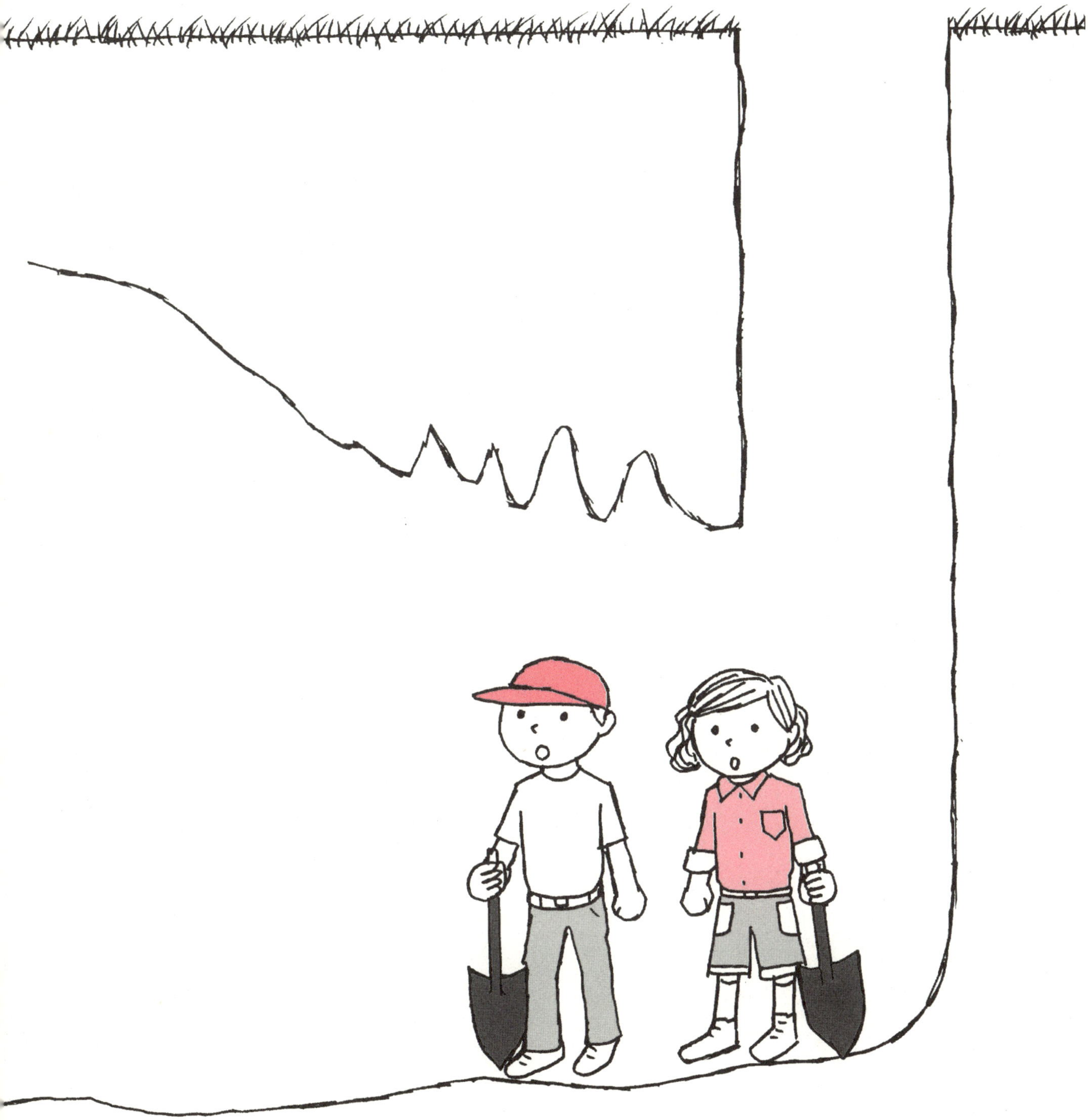

50 Drawing Something Creative
Something Heavy

■ What are they pulling?

Komondor

Komondor

Problem Solving

Missing a Tire

My bike isn't moving. Can you help?

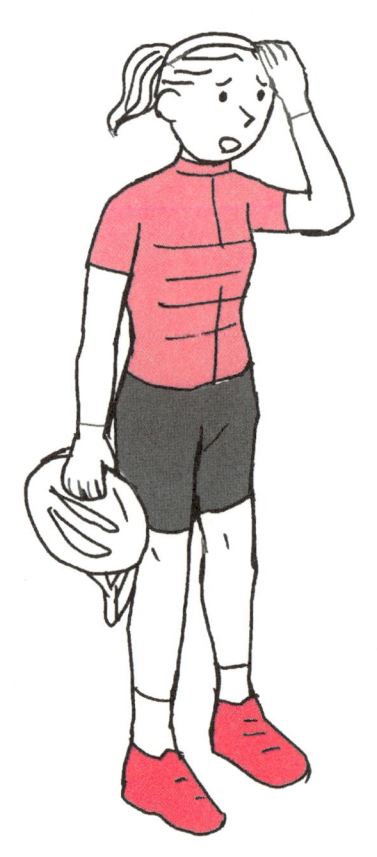

To parents: Starting with this activity, each picture shows a problem. Your child will add something to the picture to solve the problem.

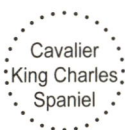

Cavalier King Charles Spaniel

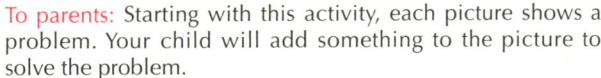

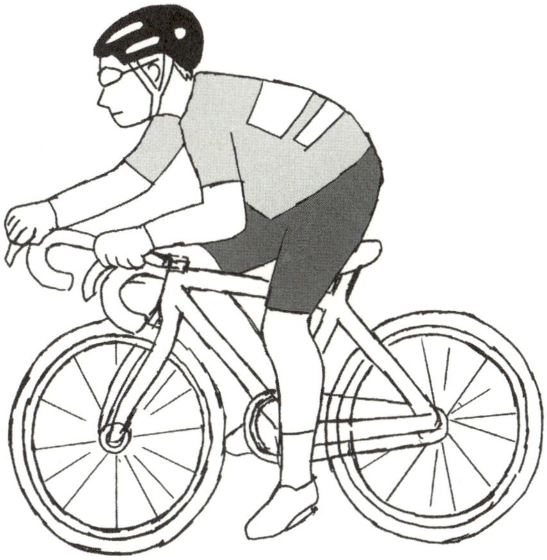

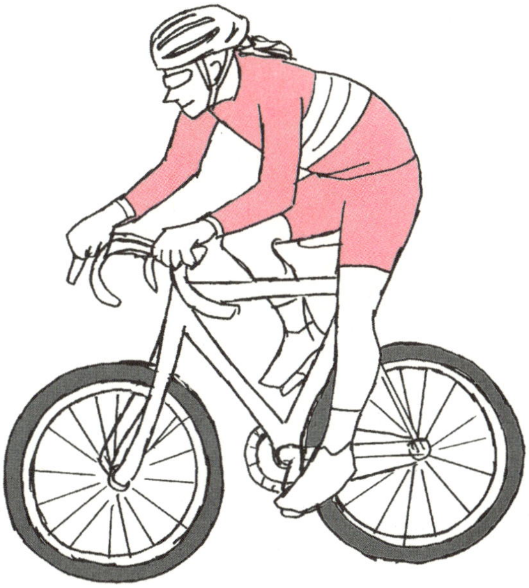

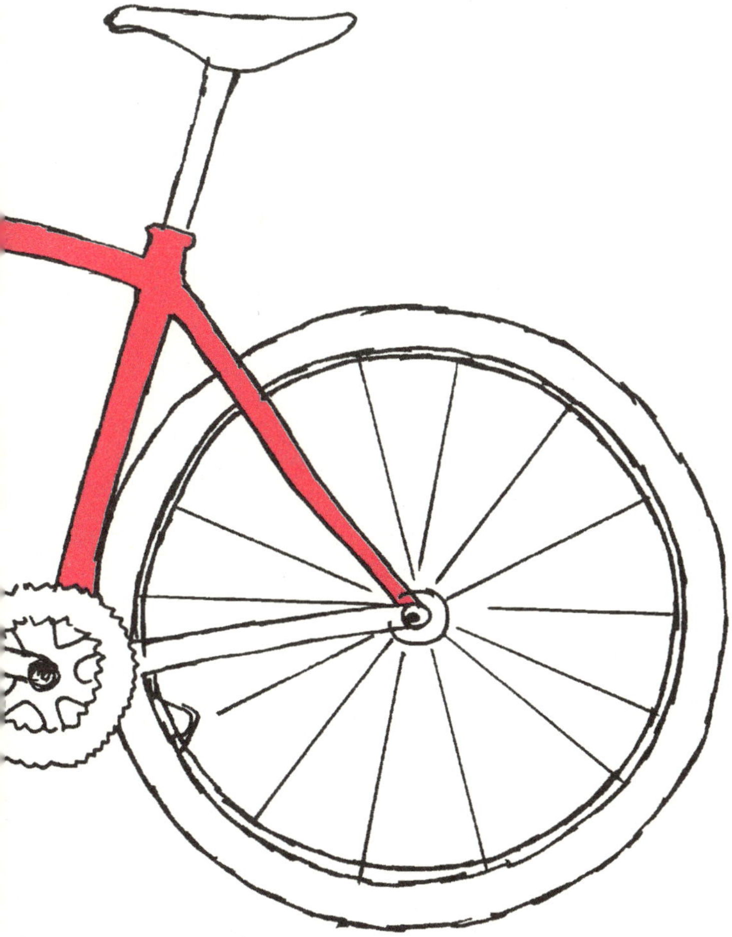

52

Problem Solving

Missing Lines

Some of the fishing lines are missing. Can you help?

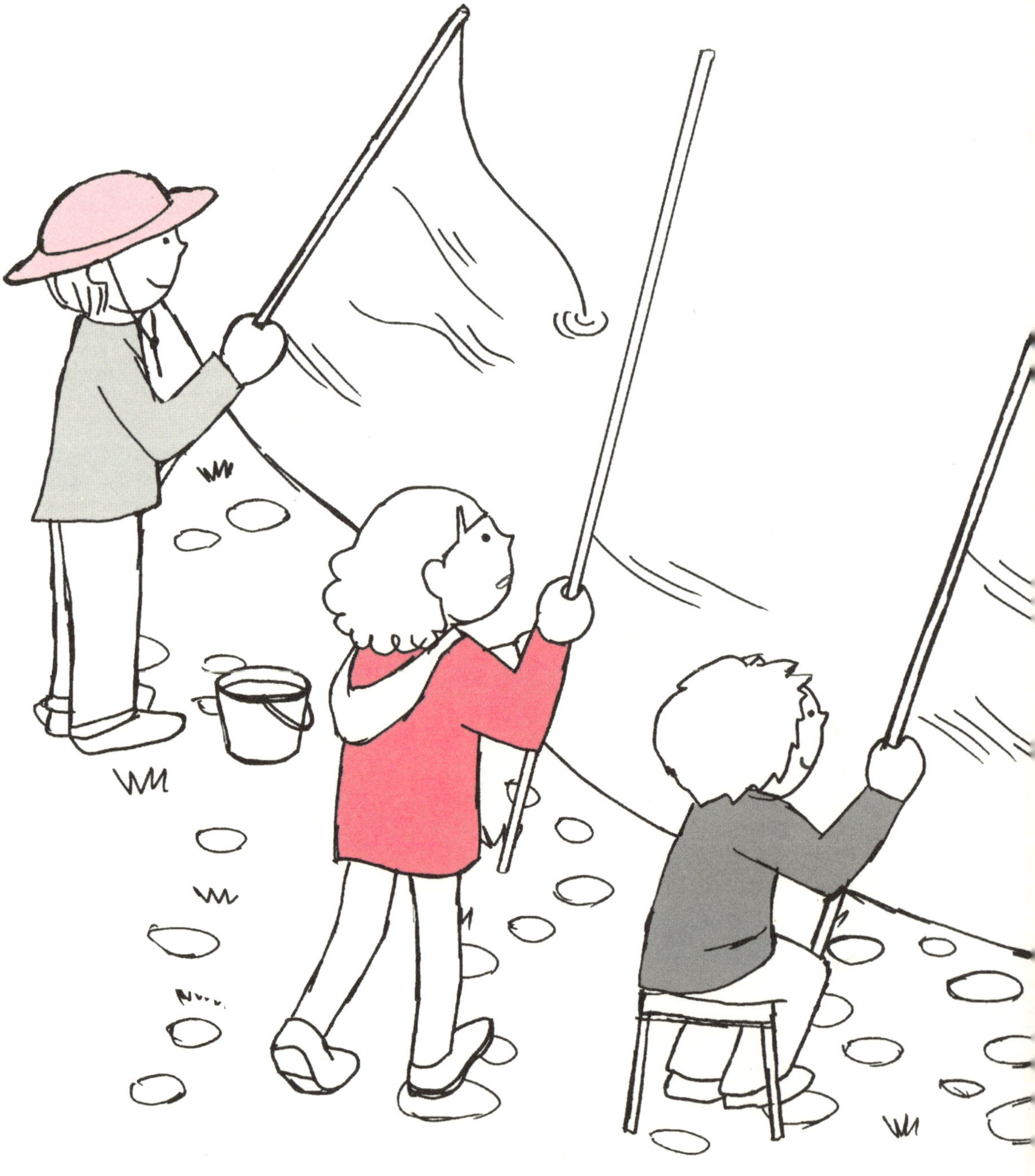

To parents: If your child has difficulty, point to the fishing rods in the picture that have lines. Then ask your child what the other fishing rods are missing.

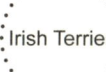

Irish Terrier

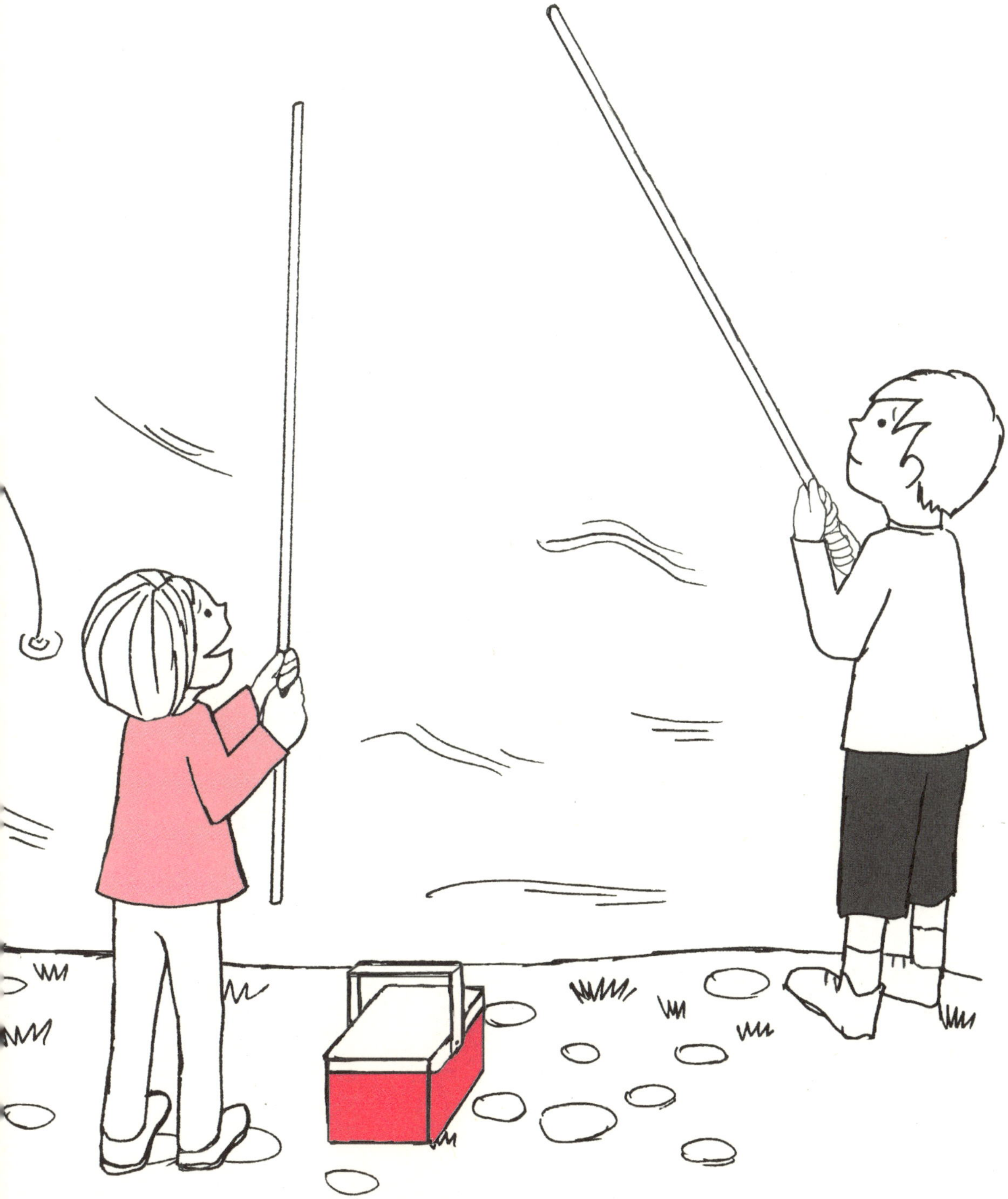

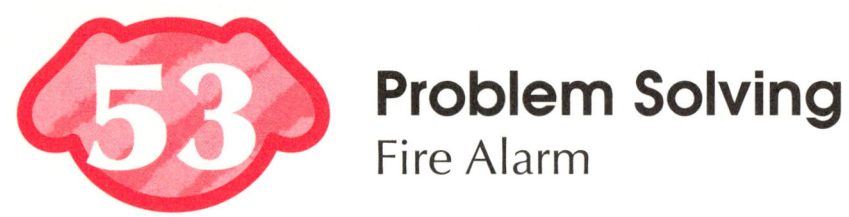

53 Problem Solving
Fire Alarm

Can you help put out the fire?

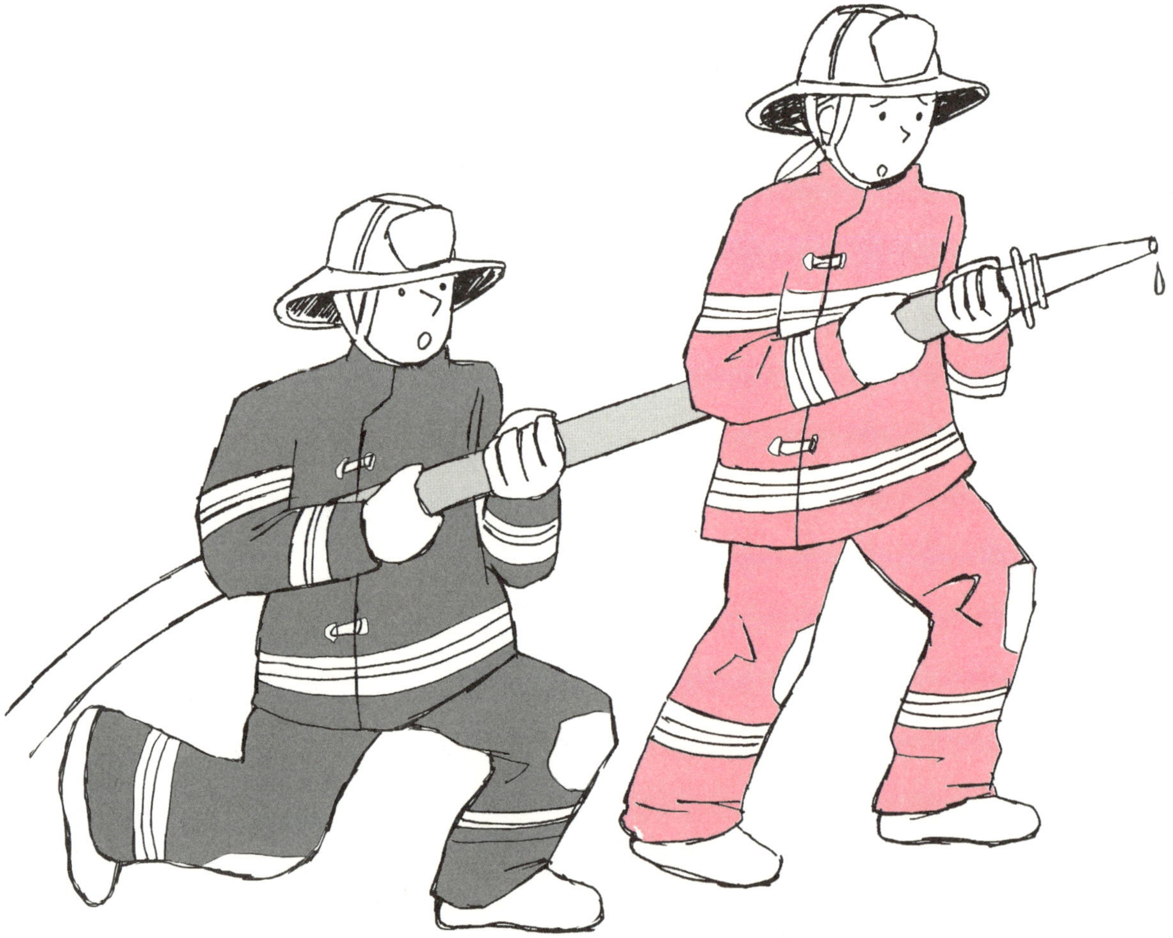

American Bulldog

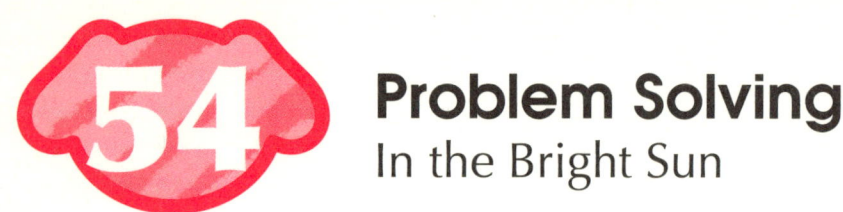

54 Problem Solving
In the Bright Sun

Can you help protect the children from the bright sun?

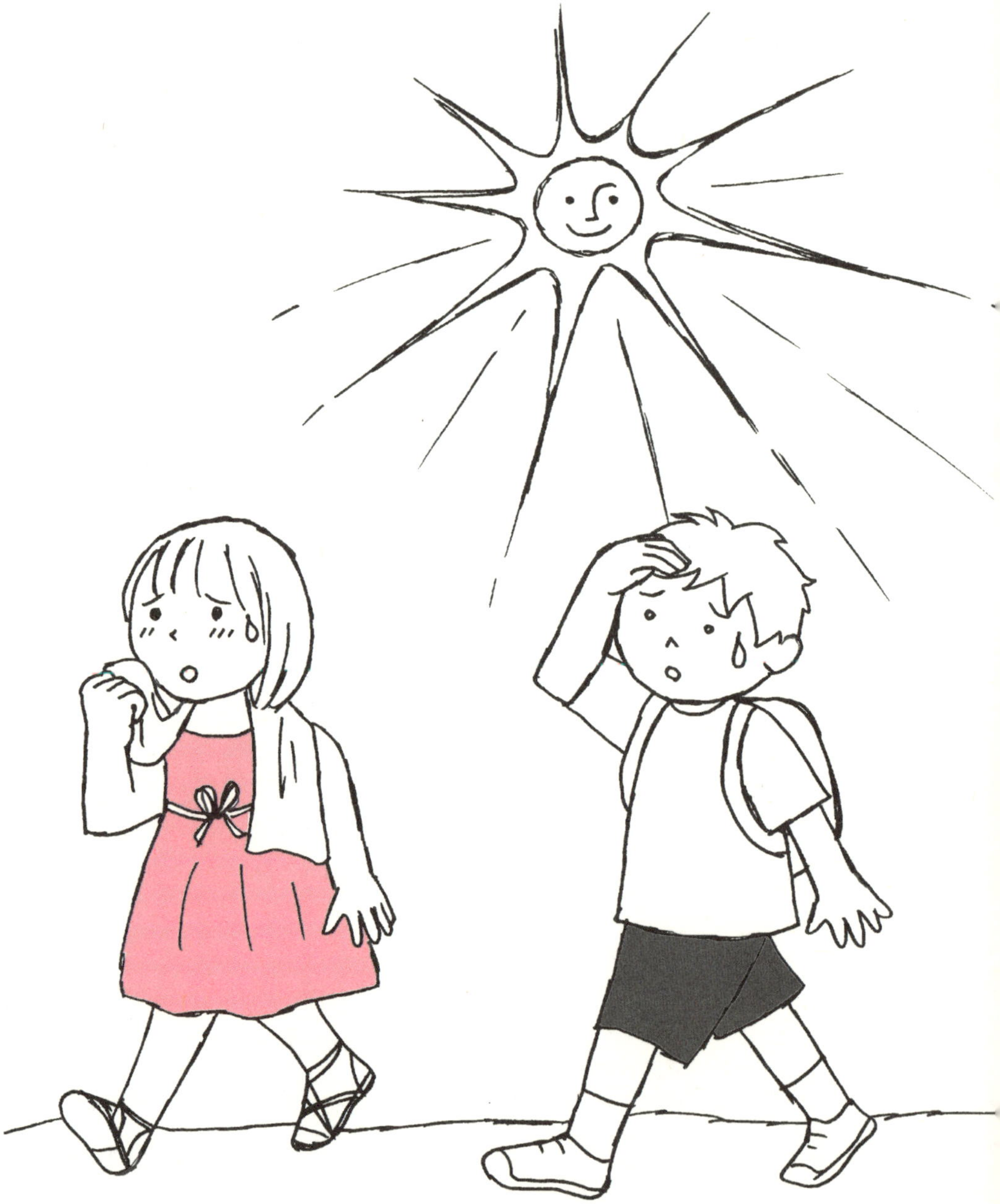

To parents: If your child has difficulty, ask your child what he or she uses to stay cool in the hot summer.

Samoyed

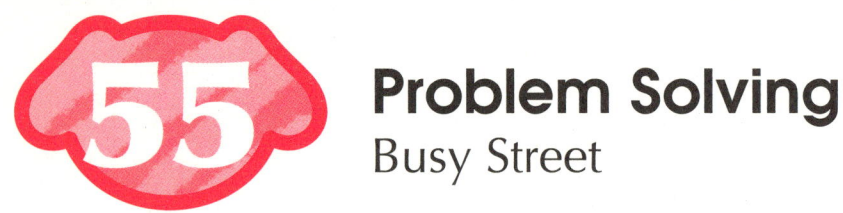

55 Problem Solving

Busy Street

Can you help the boy cross the street?

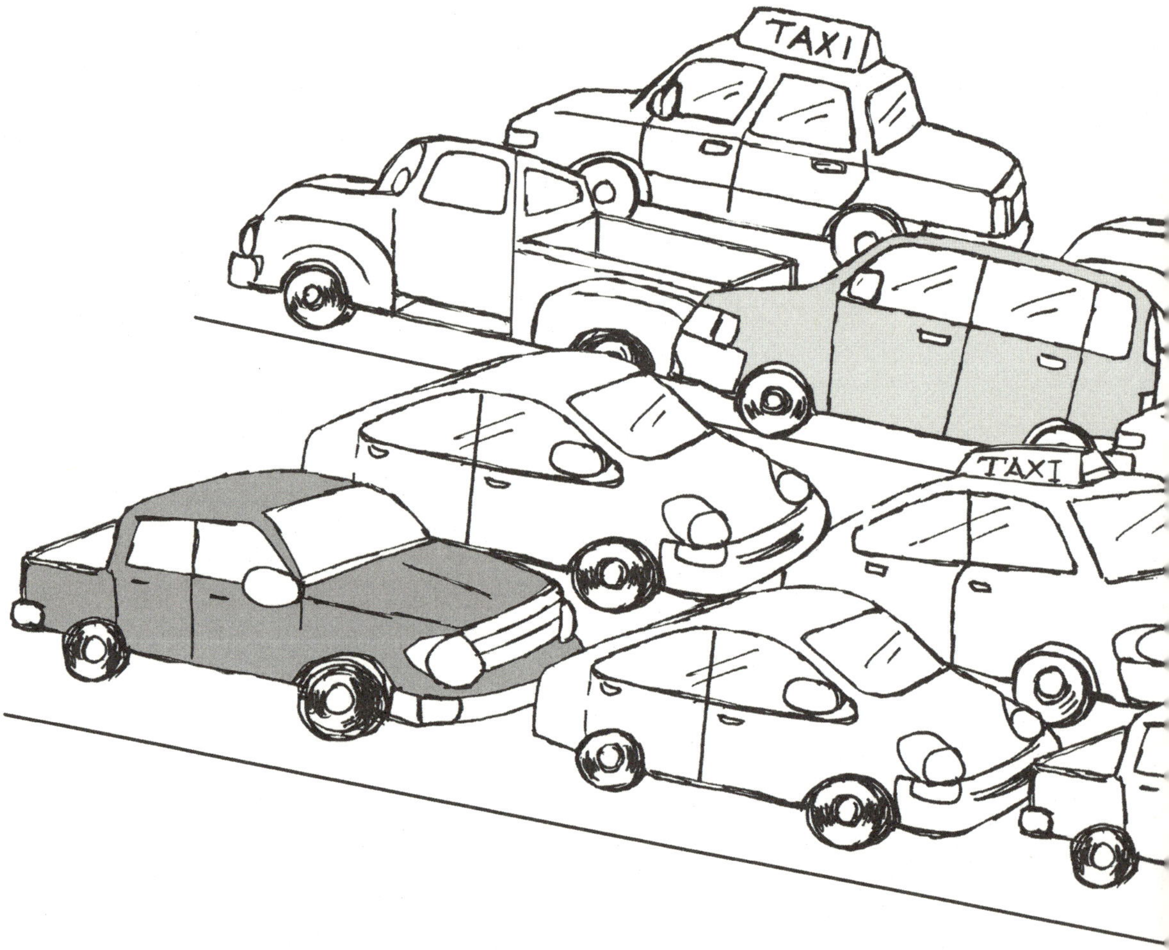

To parents: If your child has difficulty, remind him or her that there is no single correct response.

English Pointer

56

Problem Solving

SOS

Help me get down this mountain!

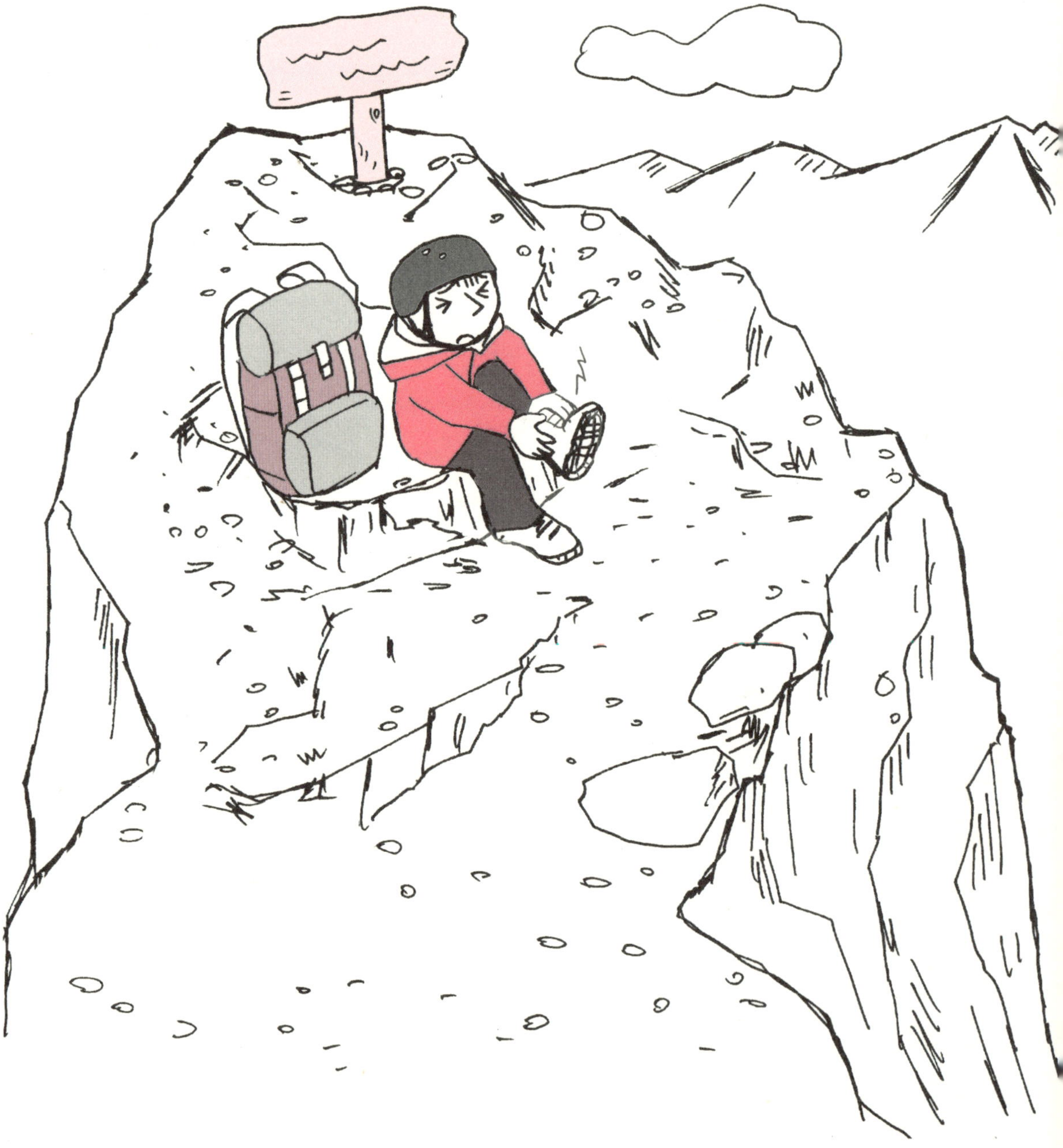

To parents: As an added challenge, encourage your child to think of several solutions before choosing one to draw.

Newfoundland

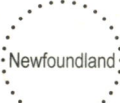

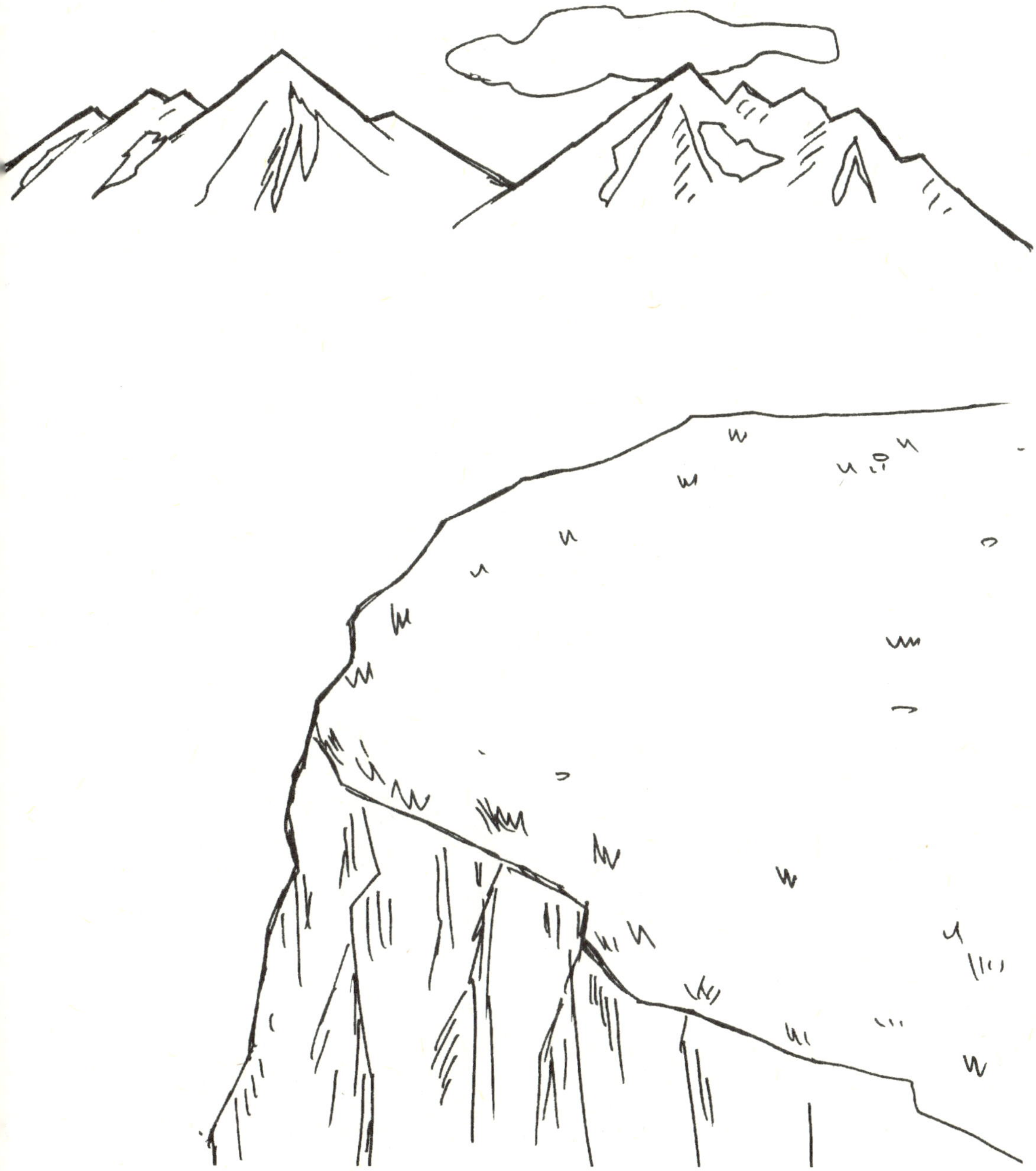

57 Problem Solving
Up on the Roof

The ball is stuck on the roof. Can you help get it?

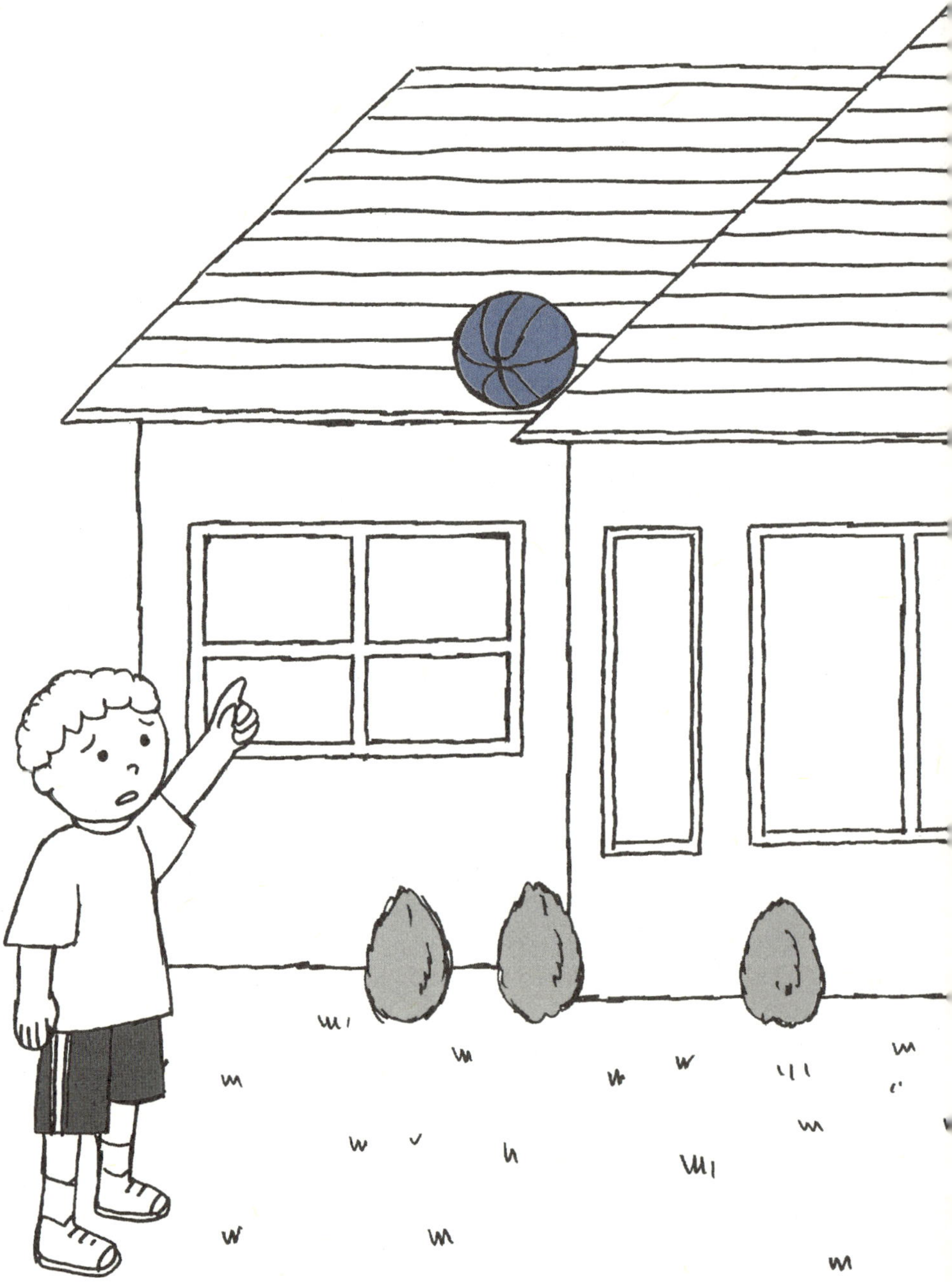

To parents: Remember that your child's drawing does not need to show something that can happen in real life.

Saluki

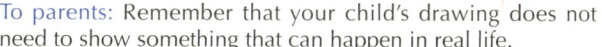

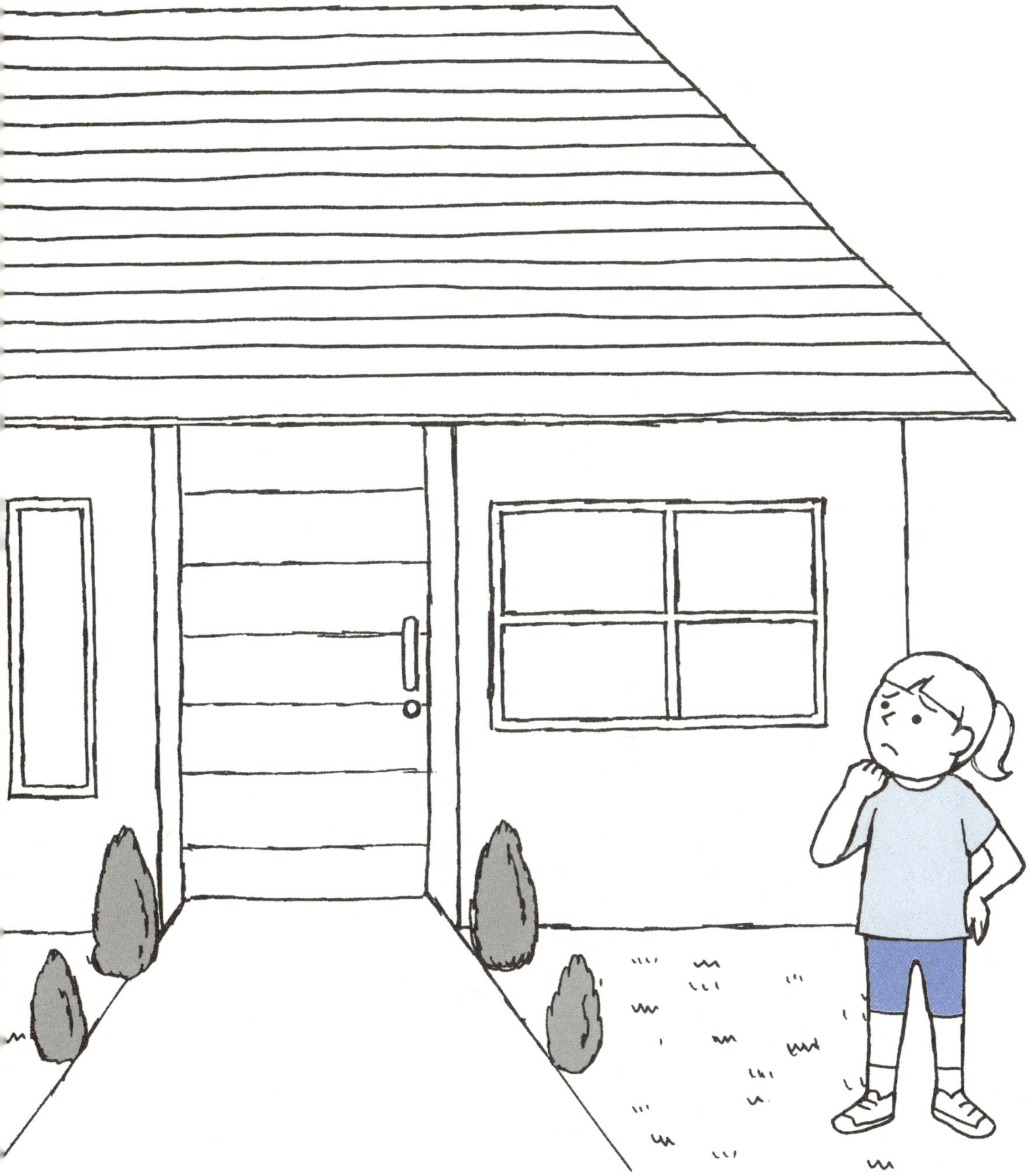

■ Save the zebra!

Rhodesian
Ridgeback

59 Problem Solving
Stuck Car

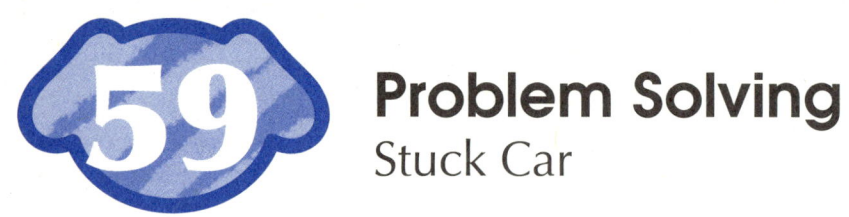

The car is stuck in the hole. Can you help get it out?

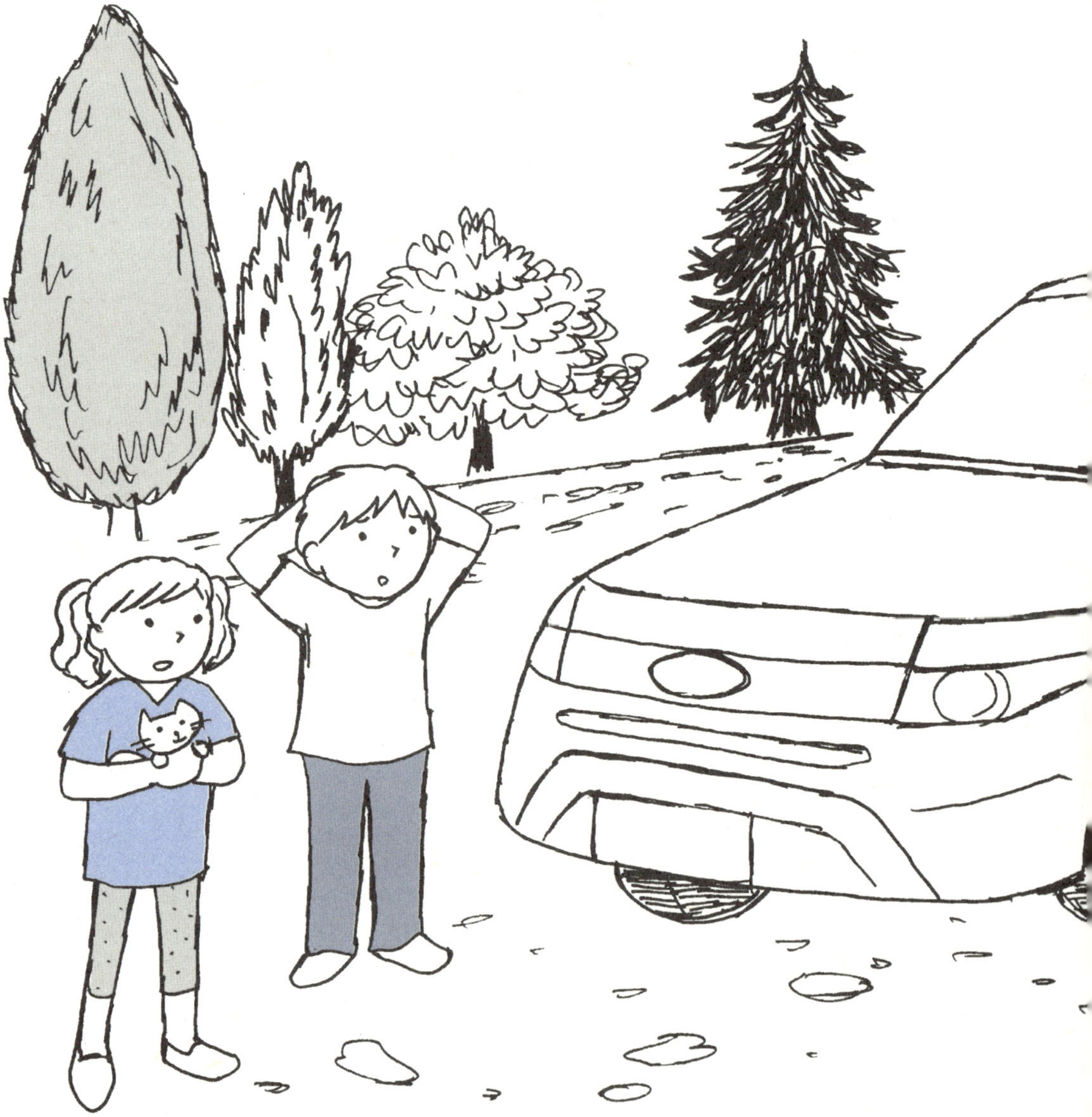

To parents: If your child has difficulty, talk about general ways to solve the problem. For example, one approach is to push the car.

Toy Fox
Terrier

Problem Solving
Dog in Danger

■ Stop the dog from falling into the hole.

American
Foxhound

61

Problem Solving

Gust of Wind

Save my letters from blowing away!

Miniature Bull Terrier

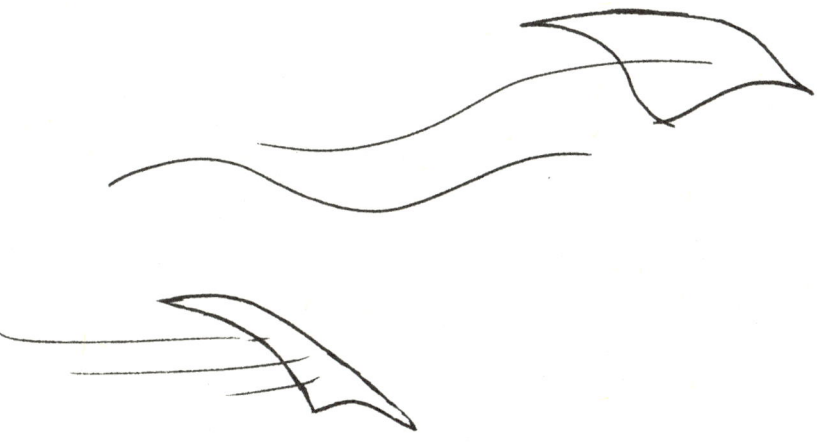

62 Problem Solving
Hanging On

Help me drop from the tree safely!

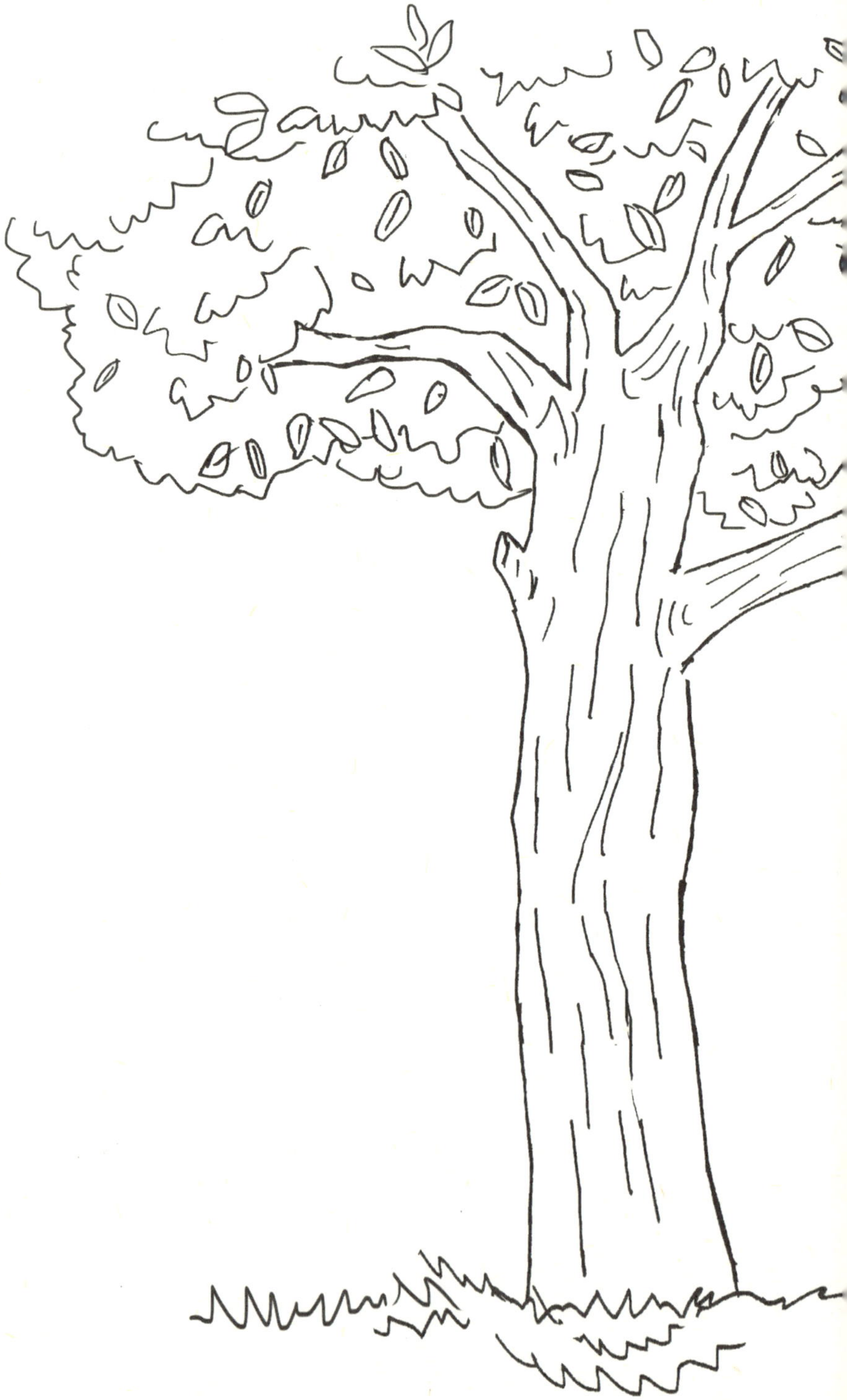

To parents: As an added challenge, encourage your child to think of several solutions before choosing one to draw.

Chinese Crested Dog

Problem Solving
Out of Reach

■ Help me reach the key!

Chow Chow

Sample Responses

There are no right or wrong answers for the activities in this book. However, descriptions of sample responses are provided below. These are provided as a guide if your child needs support completing the activities.

1 Color the apples red.
2 Color the lion cubs yellow.
3 Color the steaks brown.
4 Color the bananas yellow and the oranges orange.
5 Color the sunflowers yellow and the roses red.
6 Color the alligators green and the hippos brown.
7 Color the tropical birds any color.
8 Color the beams of light any color or colors.
9 Color the hats any color or colors.
10 Color the toy blocks any color or colors.
11 Finish drawing stripes on the tiger on the left-hand page.
12 Add any number of dots to the two giraffes without them.
13 Add a wavy line pattern to the undecorated plate.
14 Add a checkered pattern to the flag.
15 Add a pattern to the card in the right-hand page. Choose from the patterns on the other cards or develop a new one.
16 Add patterns to the pants and towel. Choose from the patterns on the other clothing or develop new ones.
17 Decorate the cake on the right-hand page. Choose from the designs shown on the other cakes or develop new ones.
18 Add patterns to the mugs. You may wish to create one matching pair.
19 Decorate the fish. Add the same pattern to each fish or make each one different.
20 Decorate the cars. Add the same pattern to each car or make each one different.
21 Draw one street for each house that does not have one.
22 Draw different sizes of bubbles in the air.
23 Draw more balls in the air between the coach and the children. You may want to draw one in a child's hands.
24 Add three or four more fish swimming in the sea.
25 Draw a sand castle on the right-hand page. Copy one of the others shown or combine elements from all three.
26 Draw a potato and a carrot in the refrigerator.
27 Draw a mountain range on the horizon.
28 Draw a soccer ball about to go in to the goal, past the goalie.
29 Draw a big spout from the whale's head.
30 Draw a long, curvy path like in a maze.
31 Draw two red dotted lines in one circle. Draw three black pentagons in the other circle.
32 Add squares for windows and a rectangle for the door.
33 Draw a triangle on top of each shape. Color the tip of each triangle black.
34 Turn each shape into a banana or a strawberry by adding lines or dots. Color the banana yellow and the strawberry red.

35 Draw the hedgehog's head, legs, and tail along the bottom of the shape. Draw spines on the top of the shape.
36 Draw a handle along the bottom of the shape, so that the existing shape forms bristles.
37 On each door, draw a circle for a knob and a square for a window.
38 Draw an animal's face such as a dog or fox under the shapes.
39 Draw a mast and sail to create a boat or decorate the shape with a pattern to create a bowl.
40 Draw buildings, tree trunks, or juice cartons.
41 Draw a sunny-side up egg, a steak, or French toast.
42 Draw a teddy bear, a book, or a video game in the chest.
43 Draw fish, an empty can, or an imaginary creature.
44 Draw a man, a woman, or a group of circus performers.
45 Draw a self-portrait, a parent's portrait, a friend's portrait, or an animal's face.
46 Draw a double rainbow or a full-circle rainbow.
47 Draw a big gorilla, a giant snake, or an imaginary creature like a dragon.
48 Draw a jungle, palm trees, or modern buildings.
49 Draw a nest of a new species of animal, a large underground lake, or gold mines.
50 Draw an elephant, a whale, or a dinosaur.
51 Draw a tire for the bike.
52 Draw lines for the fishing rods.
53 Draw water from the hose.
54 Draw hats, sunglasses, or parasols for the children.
55 Draw a traffic light, an overhead bridge, or a police officer.
56 Draw a bridge across the canyon, a party of hikers, or a helicopter hovering above the mountain.
57 Draw a wooden ladder, a butterfly net, or other balls.
58 Draw a fence between the lion and the zebra, a net over the lion, or fresh meat in front of the lion.
59 Draw sand to fill in the hole, a long rope to pull the car, or a tow truck.
60 Draw a board to cover the hole, a bone in front of the dog, or a leash on the dog.
61 Draw a net to catch the letters, draw the windows closed, or draw a stone as a paperweight.
62 Draw a ladder, a couch, or a friend reaching out his or her hand.
63 Draw a walking stick, an umbrella, or a magnet tied to the end of a rope.